EXTREME
LONGEVITY

DISCOVERING EARTH'S OLDEST ORGANISMS ≫

KAREN LATCHANA KENNEY

TWENTY-FIRST CENTURY BOOKS / MINNEAPOLIS

TO MY DEAR SON, MAXIMILIAN

Twenty-First Century Books
A division of Lerner Publishing Group, Inc.
241 First Avenue North
Minneapolis, MN 55401 USA

For reading levels and more information, look up this title at www.lernerbooks.com.

Main body text set in Adobe Garamond Pro 11/15.
Typeface provided by Adobe Systems.

Library of Congress Cataloging-in-Publication Data

Names: Kenney, Karen Latchana, author.
Title: Extreme longevity : discovering Earth's oldest organisms / Karen Latchana
    Kenney.
Description: Minneapolis : Twenty-First Century Books, [2018] | Audience: Ages
    13–18. | Audience: Grades 9 to 12. | Includes bibliographical references and index.
Identifiers: LCCN 2017044278 (print) | LCCN 2017048880 (ebook) |
    ISBN 9781541524781 (eb pdf) | ISBN 9781512483727 (lb : alk. paper)
Subjects: LCSH: Longevity—Juvenile literature. | Animals—Longevity—Juvenile
    literature. | Physiology—Juvenile literature. | Aging—Genetic aspects—Juvenile
    literature.
Classification: LCC RA776.75 (ebook) | LCC RA776.75 .K4635 2018 (print) |
    DDC 571.8/79—dc23
LC record available at https://lccn.loc.gov/2017044278

Manufactured in the United States of America
1-43366-33178-3/28/2018

CONTENTS

SPECIAL THANKS

This book developed through numerous interviews with scientists working with long-lived organisms around the world—from throughout the United States to Canada, Denmark, Italy, and New Zealand. I thank them for sharing their extensive knowledge with me and contributing photographs for use in this book. Their studies and remarkable findings remind us that nature still has many mysteries waiting to be discovered. They include the following:

- **DR. STEVEN N. AUSTAD** of the University of Alabama–Birmingham
- **DR. FERDINANDO BOERO** of the University of Salento in Lecce, Italy
- **DR. ALISON CREE** of the University of Otago in New Zealand
- **DR. MICHAEL C. GRANT, DR. JEFFRY B. MITTON, AND DR. YAN LINHART** of the University of Colorado in Boulder
- **DR. MADS PETER HEIDE-JØRGENSEN** of the Greenland Institute of Natural Resources in Nuuk

- **DR. SALLY LEYS** of the University of Alberta in Canada
- **DR. JULIUS NIELSEN** at the University of Copenhagen in Denmark
- **DR. JOÃO PEDRO DE MAGALHÃES** at the Institute of Ageing and Chronic Disease of the University of Liverpool in the United Kingdom
- **DR. DANIEL E. MARTINEZ** of Pomona College in California
- **DR. KIM PRAEBEL** of the Norwegian College of Fishery Science in Tromsø, Norway
- **DR. PAMELA REID** of the University of Miami Rosenstiel School of Marine and Atmospheric Science in Florida
- **DR. PAUL ROGERS** of the Western Aspen Alliance and Utah State University in Logan, Utah
- **DR. LEONEL STERNBERG** of the University of Miami College of Arts and Sciences in Florida

INTRODUCTION

THE WHALE THAT GOT AWAY

It's springtime 1890 in the icy Beaufort Sea, near the northern tip of the world. From their wooden steamship, whalers watch for massive black humps rising above shifting floes of thick Arctic ice. They listen for loud whooshing sounds—the sound of bowhead whales taking breaths before diving back down into the deep.

When the hunters spot a whale in the distance, a few of the men climb down into a small wooden boat to get in close. One whaler takes a shot from a shoulder-mounted gun, hoping for a direct hit.

The gun, a bomb lance harpoon, fires a bomb lance—a metal dart with an explosive tip. It slices through the air and penetrates the thick blubber beneath the whale's skin. Lodged there in bone, the tip explodes inside the whale. But the explosion does not kill the animal as it was meant to do. The whalers watch in defeat as the injured bowhead silently slips back beneath the icy water.

This underwater photo shows a bowhead whale off the eastern coast of Baffin Island, a Canadian island in the Arctic Ocean.

The whalers continue their hunt. They will never know the fate of the injured whale nor that it will outlive them, surviving in the Arctic for more than one hundred years.

HUNTING BOWHEADS

Whaling ships—launched from Europe, North America, and Asia—once ruled Arctic waters. From the seventeenth century through the nineteenth century, thousands of whalers made the dangerous trip north, navigating their ships through ice floes that could crush them at any moment. They hunted different kinds of whales, but the bowhead was a prized catch. Whalers melted down the bowhead's incredibly thick blubber into golden brown whale oil. One adult bowhead yielded up to 6,000 gallons (22,712 L) of the valuable oil—more than could be extracted from any other kind of whale. In the eighteenth and nineteenth centuries, before the development of electric lights, wealthy

In addition to hunting long-lived bowheads, whalers hunted other types of whales around the world. A British artist made this painting of whalers in the South Pacific Ocean in 1836. Whaling was dangerous work, and in this painting, a whale upends the whaleboat, throwing the hunters into the sea.

people burned whale oil in lanterns to illuminate their homes and businesses. Mechanics used the oil to lubricate axles, gears, and other machine parts.

Whalers also removed thin, flexible plates called baleen from the mouths of bowheads. Whales use these long plates to filter plankton, small fish, and other food from the water. In the nineteenth century, manufacturers used baleen to make fashion accessories, such as umbrella handles, hoops worn inside women's skirts, and stays (stiffeners) for women's corsets.

In the 1860s and 1870s, the whaling industry began to decline. By then US and European companies were drilling for petroleum to convert it into lubricating oils, kerosene, and other fuels—all much cheaper than whale oil. By this time bowheads and other whales were harder to find. Whalers had killed so many bowheads that the species was nearly extinct—almost gone from Earth forever. Historians estimate that before the seventeenth century, about thirty thousand to fifty thousand bowheads lived in the world's seas. By the early 1920s, only about three thousand bowheads remained. Other whale species were equally threatened.

Even though petroleum products had replaced whale oil for many uses, whale hunting continued. Manufacturers turned whale oil into soap and explosives and made whalebones into fertilizer. People in some northern regions, such as the Arctic, Japan, and Scandinavia, ate whale meat. With whale stocks around the world in peril, fifteen nations sought to protect the animals from overhunting and extinction. In 1946 they created the International Whaling Commission (IWC). More nations joined the commission later in its history. At first, the organization set out only to regulate the whaling industry. It set quotas, or limits, on the number of whales that commercial hunters could kill each year. Later in the twentieth century, conservationists and others called for an end to the commercial killing of whales. Meanwhile, the commission switched from regulating whale hunting to protecting

THE GIFT OF THE WHALE

Inupiat legend says that bowheads choose to give themselves to certain whaling crews. They look for clean umiaks (traditional sealskin-covered wood boats)—a sign that the hunters are respectful people who take care of their boats and will share their catch with everyone in their community. The whales want to give the gift of their lives to hunters who will honor their bodies and treat them with respect.

This legend is central to the Inupiat people, whose ancestors have lived in the Arctic for at least four thousand years. Their territory in northern and northwestern Alaska is a land of few natural resources, so bowhead hunts are important to their survival. The whales feed community members. And the traditional hunts unite people, who gather to prepare for hunts, cut and distribute the whale's body, and celebrate with feasts. They use many parts of the whale, from its baleen to make baskets to its nutrient-rich skin, blubber, organs, and meat for food. Inupiat whalers also give samples of whale tissue to biologists, who use the materials to study the animals' health, how they age, and how they reproduce.

whales. In 1982 it banned commercial whaling altogether. Not all nations signed onto the ban, however. Norway, Iceland, and Japan still hunt whales, in defiance of the global ban.

The commission does make some exceptions to its ban on whale hunting. It allows certain indigenous (native) groups that have traditionally hunted whales for food to continue to do so. One of these groups is the Inupiat people of Alaska, who eat bowhead whale blubber, meat, and skin, as their ancestors have for thousands of years. Out of respect for this ancient cultural practice, the commission allows Inupiats to hunt bowhead whales. But they must adhere to quotas. The commission allows eleven Inupiat communities in Alaska to kill up to 0.5 percent of the bowhead whale population each year. Since these kills amount to fewer bowheads than are born each year, the bowhead population continues to grow.

THE BOMB LANCE FRAGMENTS

Inupiat bowhead hunts have led to some surprising scientific discoveries. One major discovery occurred in 2007 near Barrow, Alaska, the northernmost town of the United States. It was May, the time of year when bowheads migrate from the south to feed in the eastern Beaufort Sea. Upon sighting a whale, a group of Inupiat whalers left their camp at the edge of a floe, where ice secured to land meets open water. Using a bomb lance harpoon, very similar to those used in the 1890s, the whalers killed a 50-ton (45 t) bowhead. They hauled it onto the ice. As they carved through the blubber with a chain saw, they hit something hard embedded in a bone near the whale's neck. The material was not part of the whale—it was metal. The whalers had found fragments of a bomb lance—but not the type of bomb lance that twenty-first-century Inupiat hunters use. The fragments were very old.

The hunters work with many biologists who study bowhead whales. So they contacted Craig George, a wildlife biologist with the North Slope Borough Department of Wildlife Management in Barrow, to tell him of their discovery. He went to the site and studied

In the late nineteenth century, this type of bomb lance—part of a bomb lance harpoon system patented by US weapons maker Ebenezer Pierce in 1879—wounded a whale in the Beaufort Sea. More than one hundred years later, in 2007, hunters succeeded in killing the same whale.

the bomb lance fragments. He says, "I knew immediately that [the bomb lance] was quite old by its shape." George sent the fragments to John Bockstoce, curator of the New Bedford Whaling Museum in Massachusetts. Bockstoce determined that the fragments came from a type of bomb lance patented (registered by the inventor with the government) in 1879 and likely made in a New Bedford factory. New Bedford, a coastal city on the Atlantic Ocean, was once a major whaling center—the departure point for many Arctic whaling voyages. Bockstoce believed the bomb lance had hit the whale around 1890.

Knowing the age of the bomb lance gave researchers a good idea of the bowhead's age. Assuming 1890 as the date when the whale had been harpooned with this weapon, the whale lived another 117 years before the Inupiat hunters killed it in 2007. Most likely, the whale was an adult in 1890, since whalers never hunted young bowheads. If it had been born in 1877, it was 130 years old when it died. It might have been born even earlier and lived even longer. Whatever the whale's precise age, the bomb lance fragments were clues that bowheads don't just watch years pass, they may see centuries tick by.

DATING WILD THINGS

A bowhead's life is long, but even this whale doesn't have the most extreme life span found in nature. Other organisms live just as long or longer. Some even seem to defy death. These beings include both plants and animals—from mammals and fish to pond creatures, reptiles, and ancient tree colonies. Certain jellyfish can even regenerate completely, reorganizing their cells into new jellyfish. And some animals seem immune to common old-age diseases. Biologists are discovering that nature finds different ways to trick time.

Aging is the gradual breakdown of the living body. For humans, that means gray hair, wrinkles, stiff joints, and diseases such as Alzheimer's or many kinds of cancer. But why does aging happen? Human and other animal bodies have built-in mechanisms for

Adult mayflies have extremely short lives. They emerge from the water, reproduce, and die—in some cases, within a few hours. However, prior to becoming adults, they spend one year underwater in the nymph stage.

repairing damaged cells, so why do they stop working? And why do some creatures live so long while others have very short lives?

Adult mayflies are on the short end of the spectrum. After spending a year or more living underwater as nymphs, an early stage in the life of certain insects, they become adults that live for only hours or a few days. But another kind of insect—the queen (egg-laying female) of an African mound-building termite colony—can live for sixty years. Tiny saltwater worms called gastrotriches, measuring less than 0.04 inches (1 mm) long, may spend the shortest time on Earth. Their entire life span, from birth to death, is only three days to three weeks. On the other end of the spectrum, the tiny hydra, a soft-bodied water animal, might actually be able to live forever.

Biologists have observed that larger creatures, such as bowhead whales and giant tortoises, tend to live longer than smaller ones, but they aren't sure why. There are some long-lived tiny creatures, though, such as the naked mole rat. This rodent can live for more than two decades—about four times as long as mice of the same size.

A HUMAN'S LIFE SPAN

The average human lives less than a century—about 79 years—yet some people have lived well past 100. The record holder was a Frenchwoman, Jeanne Louise Calment, who lived 122 years and 164 days before her death in 1997. A centenarian lives to be 100 to 109, and people who live to be 110 or older are supercentenarians. This exclusive club had only thirty-nine members in the entire world in 2018. Some recent members were born in the nineteenth century and died in the twenty-first century, so they lived in three different centuries!

Since the mid-nineteenth century, humans have been living longer. In fact, the average human life span has doubled in the past two hundred years, from about thirty-five in 1817 to seventy-nine in 2017. This increase stems from advances in public health, primarily during the twentieth century. That's when researchers developed dozens of vaccines, which prevent deadly diseases and reduce infant deaths. Twentieth-century medical researchers also devised treatments for infections and diseases. In wealthy nations, communities built sanitation systems, which pipe clean water to homes and businesses and remove human waste to sewage treatment plants. These systems prevent the spread of disease through contaminated water.

Jeanne Louise Calment posed for this photo in 1988, when she was 113. She lived to be 122—the oldest documented human life span.

Some biologists believe that our species has reached the upper limit of its life span. A 2016 study by molecular biologist Jan Vijg and his colleagues at the Albert Einstein College of Medicine in New York shows that the human life span began to plateau, or level off, in the mid-1990s. The study suggests that the average life span won't continue to lengthen. But other biologists don't buy this idea. They note that life spans in some wealthy, industrialized nations—such as Japan (85 years), Italy (82.2 years), and France (81.8 years)—are still growing longer. And future medical discoveries and technology might extend the human life span even more.

This rat's life span pokes holes in current theories about aging. Is there even a pattern to aging? If so, what's the key to slowing it down?

Biologists around the world are figuring out pieces of the longevity puzzle, and they're looking at some extraordinary animals for clues. But studying a wild animal's life span isn't easy, especially if it lives for many decades—sometimes much longer than the humans who are studying it. If an animal is small enough to fit into a laboratory or a zoo, researchers can observe and study its life from birth to death. But some of the longest-living creatures are too big for human-made enclosures. Some also survive in extreme conditions such as the frigid Arctic seas, hidden under thick ice.

Often discovering an organism's longevity starts with a bit of serendipity—a lucky accident that trained eyes see as a clue. The clue leads to questions, studies, and analysis, and hopefully a rare find, such as the long life span of the bowhead whale. And a discovery like that leads to even more questions, such as these: Why do some organisms live so long? And what other organisms have been living on Earth for centuries or even thousands of years?

CHAPTER 1

BOWHEAD WHALES: SLOW, COLD, AND VERY OLD

Inupiat whalers have been watching bowheads for centuries, observing their migration patterns. The whales swim north in summer, when temperatures rise and the Arctic Ocean has less ice and more open water. They move south in winter, when temperatures drop and the Arctic ice sheet expands. The Inupiats also observe the whales' growth and behaviors, even noticing specific whales within the population. Before researchers had proof to confirm the observations, Inupiats told stories of seeing the same whales over several human generations. They said that bowheads live "two human lifetimes." The 2007 discovery of bomb lance fragments showed the Inupiat stories could be true.

The discovery of a bomb lance that could be traced to a specific factory and time period was extremely rare. This bomb lance and other old harpoon tips are evidence that bowheads live an incredibly long time. But accurate and precise estimates of a bowhead's age can come only from scientific study. That starts with observing bowhead whales in their natural habitat—the Arctic.

MEGAMAMMALS OF THE ARCTIC

Slowly swimming beneath the packed ice of the cold Arctic waters is one of the largest mammals on Earth—the bowhead whale. A bowhead's enormous black-and-white head makes up one-third of its body length. Named for its arched mouth, which looks like a bow used to fire arrows, the bowhead has the largest mouth of any animal in the world. It can measure up to 10 feet (3 m) across, and its tongue alone weighs 1 ton (0.9 t)!

Each side of a bowhead's upper jaw contains about three hundred baleen plates. The bowhead uses these long plates to filter close to

110 tons (100 t) of zooplankton (small sea animals that drift with ocean currents) from the water every year. This food gives the whale enough energy to grow to 45 to 60 feet (14 to 18 m) long and weigh from 75 to 100 tons (68 to 91 t). Up to half of that weight comes from an insulating layer of blubber that can be 1.6 feet (0.5 m) thick. This layer helps the whale survive water temperatures as low as 28°F (–2°C).

The whale doesn't stay long at the ocean's surface. It spends most of its time in the mysterious, dark Arctic depths, below thick layers of ice. Whales breathe through a blowhole at the top of their heads. After taking a breath above water, a bowhead can stay submerged in a deep dive for thirty minutes or more.

Along with the extreme Arctic temperatures, the amount of time bowheads spend underwater makes the whales incredibly difficult to study. To do so, biologists travel on research vessels to tag whales at sea. When a bowhead surfaces, the researchers shoot it with a nonlethal

BIOLOGICAL BLUEPRINT: BOWHEAD WHALE

Common names: bowhead whale, bowhead, and Greenland right whale

Scientific name: *Balaena mysticetus*

Habitat: Arctic and subarctic seas

Diet: at least sixty different species of small to medium-size zooplankton

Length: 45 to 60 feet (14 to 18 m)

Weight: 75 to 100 tons (68 to 91 t)

Life span: about 211 years old (plus or minus 35 years), based on when the oldest known bowhead died

Curious adaptation: With their gigantic skulls, bowhead whales can break through sea ice at least 7.9 inches (20 cm) thick. Some Inupiat whalers report seeing bowheads break through 2-foot-thick (60 cm) sea ice.

INUPIATS TOLD STORIES OF SEEING THE SAME WHALES OVER SEVERAL HUMAN GENERATIONS. THEY SAID THAT BOWHEADS LIVE "TWO HUMAN LIFETIMES."

dart or attach a suction cup to its skin. The dart or suction cup is equipped with an electronic tag. When the whale surfaces again, the tag sends signals to a Global Positioning System (GPS) satellite. Data from the satellite goes to land-based computers. Researchers use the data to learn where whales migrate and how deep they dive. But measuring a bowhead's life span is harder. For that information, researchers look directly into the whales' eyes.

TESTING BOWHEAD EYES

Marine biologists can assess the life spans of some kinds of whales by looking at their teeth. The teeth grow new layers each year, and researchers can count the layers to find a whale's age. Researchers also measure hardened earwax that builds up in some whales' ears over time. But bowheads don't have hard teeth—they have soft baleen— and they don't have earwax either. So biologist Craig George decided to see if the pool ball–size eyeballs of bowheads could reveal their age. He wanted to use aspartic acid racemization, which involves measuring aspartic acid, a substance found in animal proteins. In whales, researchers analyze aspartic acid levels in the clear, round lenses in their eyes.

NAME GAMES

All plants and animals have common names, such as the bowhead whale or the Greenland shark. Biologists also use a scientific naming system created by Swedish botanist Carolus Linnaeus in the mid-eighteenth century. The system uses Greek- and Latin-based terms to identify each plant or animal's genus (a group of closely related organisms) and species (the specific kind within that group). For example, the scientific name for bowhead whales is *Balaena mysticetus*. *Balaena* is the genus name, and *mysticetus* is the species name.

Genus and species are the most precise classifications for living things. But these categories fall under a larger naming umbrella consisting of eight levels: domain, kingdom, phylum, class, order, family, genus, and species. You can see the hierarchy by looking at bowhead whales. They belong to the domain Eukarya—a group that includes all plants, animals, and fungi, as well as single-celled organisms called protists. Within that category, bowhead whales belong to the kingdom Animalia (the animal kingdom), the phylum Chordata (animals with backbones), the class Mammalia (mammals, which are animals that have hair or fur and nurse their young), the order Cetacea (dolphins, porpoises, and whales), the family Balaenidae (bowhead and right whales), and the genus *Balaena* (bowhead whales). The species name *Balaena mysticetus* is the specific designation for the bowhead whale. Each kind of living thing has its own species name, and members of the same species can mate with one another.

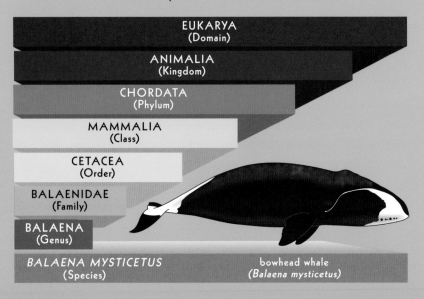

| EUKARYA (Domain) |
| ANIMALIA (Kingdom) |
| CHORDATA (Phylum) |
| MAMMALIA (Class) |
| CETACEA (Order) |
| BALAENIDAE (Family) |
| BALAENA (Genus) |
| BALAENA MYSTICETUS (Species) |

bowhead whale
(*Balaena mysticetus*)

Each lens of a bowhead whale eye has concentric layers, like the layers of an onion. The innermost layer is the nucleus, which forms when the whale is still in its mother's womb. After the nucleus forms, the aspartic acid in this layer begins to undergo chemical changes, which continue over the course of the whale's lifetime. Taking the lens from the eye of a dead bowhead, researchers can analyze the amount of aspartic acid in the nucleus to estimate how many years earlier the nucleus formed. Since it formed shortly before the animal was born, that length of time is the whale's approximate age. Aspartic acid racemization doesn't give precise results but includes a margin of error. For instance, an aspartic acid racemization age estimate of 172 years might be up to 29 years high or up to 29 years low. The margin of error increases as the age of the animal increases.

THE SHOCKING RESULTS

George had been saving bowhead eyes from whale hunts since 1978. In the late 1990s, he sent forty-eight eyes from different whales to the pioneers of aspartic acid racemization: geochemist Jeffrey Bada and his colleagues at the Scripps Institution of Oceanography in San Diego, California. Even though six of the lenses were contaminated and had to be thrown out, forty-two could be dated. The team found that most of the whales were under 100 years of age when they died. But four of the bowheads had lived much longer: 135, 159, 172, and an incredible 211 years. Even though these age estimates had margins of error, here was scientific evidence that bowhead whales could live more than two times longer than humans live.

THE RESULTS OF THE STUDY WERE CONTROVERSIAL. NOT EVERYONE BELIEVED THAT A WHALE COULD LIVE FOR SO LONG.

THE BOWHEAD'S BIGGEST THREAT

Commercial whaling was at one time the biggest threat to the bowhead whale. In the twenty-first century, another threat has taken its place. According to Mads Peter Heide-Jørgensen of the Greenland Institute of Natural Resources in Nuuk, Greenland, there is "no doubt that threat is climate change."

In the nineteenth century, humans began burning large amounts of fossil fuels (coal, oil, and natural gas) to power factories. Burning fossil fuels adds excess carbon dioxide and other gases to Earth's atmosphere. The atmosphere naturally traps the sun's heat near Earth. But large amounts of carbon dioxide trap even more heat. Because of the continued burning of fossil fuels, temperatures on Earth are rising. The higher temperatures are melting polar ice and causing sea levels to rise. The higher temperatures are also causing more extreme weather, such as devastating hurricanes and severe droughts. The oceans are also suffering. They are warming and are absorbing more carbon dioxide from the atmosphere. These changes are disrupting ocean ecosystems (communities of living things that depend on one another for survival) and harming many kinds of ocean life, including zooplankton.

What does this mean for the bowhead? Although bowhead blubber keeps the animals warm in the frigid Arctic, that layer of fat is already "causing a problem for the whales, since they cannot get rid of the heat," Heide-Jørgensen points out. "This is an increasing problem with warming sea temperatures." To adapt, bowheads are seeking cooler polar waters to compensate for the rising temperatures. But that means they are spending less time in some of the best feeding areas. Heide-Jørgensen is monitoring the bowheads through satellite tagging studies to better understand how climate change is affecting them.

That bowheads could live for more than two centuries was shocking news. The results of the study, published in 1999 in the *Canadian Journal of Zoology*, were controversial. Not everyone believed a whale could live for so long. Was there a problem with the technique? Even George was concerned. He says, "We were a little frightened when we first published [the age results]." The ages seemed too extreme, and the scientific community might not accept his results. But finding a patented harpoon tip in 2007 gave the age estimates and other evidence more credibility. Craig declared, "I think it's time to believe it."

CHAPTER 2
GREENLAND SHARKS: ARCTIC ANCIENTS

A nother ancient creature swims the Arctic—and it can live even longer than the bowhead whale, maybe even a few centuries longer. It's one of the largest carnivorous (meat-eating) fish in the world, slowly cruising the deep, cold waters of the Arctic and subarctic oceans. Meet the Greenland shark.

ICY SURVIVORS

Its dark gray skin looks like mottled stone. Its milky green eyes stare off into the distance. With its slow movements, it seems almost frozen. The Greenland shark looks old too, like a stony relic from the past.

Much about the Greenland shark is still a mystery. The animal lives under a thick layer of sea ice, so humans rarely encounter it naturally. Studying the sharks is difficult, but marine

A Greenland shark swims beneath the ice of Lancaster Sound, off the coast of Baffin Island in Canada.

biologists know that most are from 8 to 11 feet (2.5 to 3.5 m) long. Some are even longer—up to 18 feet (5.5 m). And some have weighed 2,600 pounds (1,180 kg).

Biologists have never seen a Greenland shark hunting. They are most likely scavengers, eating animals that have already died, but they may be active hunters too. To find out what Greenland sharks eat, researchers look inside the stomachs of any dead sharks they find. There, they have discovered fish, seals, squid, whales, crustaceans, birds, and even polar bears. They've found land mammals too, such as reindeer and sled dogs, which probably fell through ice into the water. Greenland sharks swim slowly—about 1.6 miles (2.6 km) an hour—so they are not high-speed killers. Biologists don't know what hunting tricks they use to catch their prey.

Like other fish, Greenland sharks take in oxygen from the water through gills at the sides of their heads. Unlike whales, they don't need to surface to breathe. Marine biologists use tag-and-release methods

BIOLOGICAL BLUEPRINT: GREENLAND SHARK

Common names: Greenland shark, gurry shark, large sleeper shark, sleeper, and sleeper shark

Scientific name: *Somniosus microcephalus*

Habitat: Arctic and North Atlantic Oceans

Diet: carnivorous—eating fish, seabirds, seals, narwhals, and other animals

Length: most 8 to 11 feet (2.5 to 3.5 m) long, some up to 18 feet (5.5 m) long

Weight: at least 2,600 pounds (1,180 kg), the largest animals likely much heavier

Life span: possibly more than five hundred years

Curious adaptation: Sharks' bodies are covered with toothlike scales called denticles. On other sharks, the denticles lie flat, but the Greenland shark's denticles are like very sharp teeth that stick straight out. Drag is a force that slows moving objects as they rub against air or water. Sharks' denticles have grooves that reduce drag, allowing sharks to glide gently and quickly through the water.

to gather information about their behavior beneath the ice. They also study dead Greenland sharks accidentally caught in nets used for scientific surveys of other fish populations.

AN UNEXPECTED COINCIDENCE

In 2010 one netted shark caught the attention of Julius Nielsen, a marine biologist and then a PhD student at the University of Copenhagen in Denmark. He was working on a research vessel near Greenland. The shark he saw was a big one, weighing more than 2,300 pounds (1,050 kg) and measuring 14.7 feet (4.5 m) long. Seeing one up close, Nielsen "became super-fascinated with this animal, especially since not much was known about them." He read a study on the growth

Marine biologist Julius Nielsen places a tracking tag under the fin of a Greenland shark while a colleague holds the shark in position beneath their research vessel. The tag will record the depth and temperature of the water the shark swims in, track how far and where the shark swims, and gather other details about its behavior and environment.

of Greenland sharks published in 1963 by Danish marine biologist Paul Marinus Hansen. The study showed the results of tagging experiments on 411 Greenland sharks throughout the 1930s and 1940s.

Biologists had caught the sharks, tagged them with numbers, and measured their lengths. If the sharks were caught again, the fisher could record each shark's identification number and growth and report it back to Hansen. Out of the 411 sharks, only 28 were caught again. In all but three cases, those who caught the sharks didn't measure them accurately.

Hansen studied the data on these three sharks. After sixteen years, one of the sharks had grown only 3 inches (8 cm). Another had grown less than 0.5 inch (1 cm) in two years, and the third had grown less than 6 inches (15 cm) in fourteen years. The results were few, but the clues were there—Greenland sharks grow incredibly slowly.

MARINE BIOLOGIST JULIUS NIELSEN: FIELDWORK IN THE ARCTIC

Julius Nielsen (*below*) has been interested in animals for as long as he can remember. When he's not studying Greenland sharks, he loves to photograph hawks feeding near his countryside home in Denmark. "I've done this kind of thing all my life," he says. "Becoming a biologist and working with animals was what I always wanted to do," says Nielsen.

His work takes him to Arctic waters three or four times a year on research vessels, where he catches, tags, and releases Greenland sharks for further study. What's it like on a research trip? "It's fun first of all!" Nielsen says. "There is a lot of waiting on these research vessels, but it's exciting being on these ships. Sometimes we wait for days and even weeks and then all of a sudden have lots of action."

Nielsen says, "We tag live sharks, using a catch-and-release process. It's nice seeing them alive and then releasing them—it's a cool part of the job." He explains why tagging sharks is so important and how it works. "We tag them, and after three or six months, the tags release to the surface and then send all recorded data to us via a satellite connection. The information we get from these tags includes the depths the sharks have occupied and the coldness of the water. We also get a GPS position on where the tag is, so we can see how far the sharks have been swimming," Nielsen explains. "We are working on analyzing these results, but preliminary data suggest that these sharks might be swimming in large groups in their deep-sea habitat."

Nielsen realized that the netted shark he had seen on the research vessel had to have been alive for a very long time to grow to be 14.7 feet (4.5 m) long.

In the fall of 2010, back at the university, Nielsen attended a lecture by Professor John F. Steffensen, who discussed Greenland sharks and their unknown life span. He said that the largest one, weighing 2,200 pounds (1,005 kg), had been caught one hundred years before. That caught the attention of Nielsen, who said, "Actually, two months ago I caught one that was bigger than that, 1,050 kilos [2,300 pounds]." This surprised his professor and further sparked Nielsen's curiosity. He decided to focus his PhD work on the biology of Greenland sharks, including their longevity.

But finding their age seemed an almost impossible task. Marine biologists normally use otoliths, also called ear stones, to date the age of bony fish. These hard bones in a bony fish's ears have growth rings that can be counted, like the rings of a tree. But sharks don't have ear stones, and much of their skeleton is made of soft cartilage, not hard bones. Some sharks have growth rings on the few hard body parts they do have, such as fins and spines. But the entire Greenland shark skeleton is made of extremely soft cartilage, which does not show growth rings. Nielsen and his team of researchers would have to get creative to figure out the Greenland shark's age.

LOOKING INSIDE THE EYES

The team decided to go with the eyes, as had been done with bowhead whales. Like the bowhead whale, the center of the Greenland shark's eye lens contains the secrets of its longevity. Proteins at the center of the lens do not change after the shark's birth. To analyze these proteins, Nielsen and his team collected the eyes of twenty-eight sharks that had been accidentally killed during scientific surveys from 2010 to 2013.

Nielsen explains that for each sample, the team first "dissected the eye and removed the eye lens. We then isolated the eye lens nucleus and removed all accumulated tissue that had been laid down over the animal's lifetime." What remained were small translucent globes, the oldest tissue found in the sharks, dating to their births.

Nielsen tried aspartic acid racemization testing on the lenses, but the results were inconclusive. This kind of testing works best on animals that have a constant body temperature over their lifetime. Whales are warm-blooded mammals. They make their own steady heat. But Greenland sharks are cold-blooded animals. Their body temperature depends on their environment. The Greenland shark's body temperature matches that of the frigid waters it lives in, from 32°F to 39°F (0°C to 4°C). Nielsen believes that this low and constantly changing body temperature distorted the test results. "The differences between young and old Greenland sharks were not as clear as was shown for whales," he says.

THE BOMB PULSE

Since they couldn't use these test results to reveal the Greenland shark's life span, Nielsen and his team could only estimate the sharks' ages. To do this, they used radiocarbon dating—also called carbon 14 dating—a technique that had worked on both whales and other shark species. The team combined two radiocarbon dating methods to make their estimates.

One radiocarbon dating method involves military history. The Cold War (1945–1991) was a time of intense political distrust, suspicion, and social, military, and economic rivalry between the United States and the Soviet Union (a union of republics that included Russia). During this era, the two countries tested nuclear weapons aboveground to show their military strength, mostly between 1955 and 1963. In 1963 the two nations and the United Kingdom signed the Limited Test Ban Treaty. It prohibited the testing of nuclear bombs in the atmosphere, in outer space, and underwater. But tests that had already occurred left a lasting mark on all living things on the planet. The tests had saturated the atmosphere with neutrons. They combined with naturally occurring hydrogen to form carbon 14. This elevated level of carbon 14 is known as the bomb pulse. Plants absorbed the excess carbon 14 from the air, and animals absorbed it when they ate those plants. The first affected were organisms on land, and then "the bomb pulse penetrated the ocean in the early 1960s," Nielsen explains. "First it went into the algae. Then bigger organisms ate the algae and incorporated the levels [of carbon 14]. Fish ate those organisms, seals and other animals ate the fish, and then Greenland sharks ate those animals, incorporating the levels."

Biologists use this spike in carbon 14 as a time marker. If they see it in the eye lens nucleus of a Greenland shark, it means the animal was born after the early 1960s. If the spike is not present, then the shark was born before the 1960s, before the bomb pulse entered the ocean. Nielsen and his team found the high carbon 14 levels of the bomb pulse in only three of the Greenland sharks in his study—and they were the smallest of the group.

THE OLDEST SHARKS

That could only mean one thing—the bigger sharks, with no bomb pulse markers, were born before the 1960s and were likely far older than fifty years. The test results were incredible, even to Nielsen. He says, "I thought that the accelerator [a measuring machine] had done something wrong! I had an idea they were old, but to learn that almost all our sharks were older than fifty years was quite surprising."

Using a different radiocarbon dating method, the shark researchers calculated the estimated ages of the twenty-five prebomb sharks. This method required quite some time to develop. First, the team gathered all the historical information they could about carbon 14 levels in the North Atlantic Ocean over the previous five hundred years. They used the data to make a statistical model (a complex mathematical equation) that calculated age estimates of the sharks older than fifty.

FINDING MING

One marine creature lives even longer than the Greenland shark—the ocean quahog (*Arctica islandica*), a type of clam. All clams are bivalves, animals that live inside two protective hard shells. By counting growth rings on the ligament (connecting tissue) that forms a hinge between the shells, biologists have learned that bivalves live long lives.

Until 2006 the oldest ocean quahog ever found was 220 years old. That year researchers from Bangor University in Wales caught an ocean quahog as part of a study in Iceland. They counted the tightly packed growth rings on the hinge ligament of one quahog and found that it was an astounding 507 years old. The researchers named it Ming, after the Ming dynasty of China. This family was in power in 1499, when the quahog was born.

Animal aging expert Steven N. Austad of the University of Alabama–Birmingham studies the ocean quahog and other animals. He was astonished to hear the news of Ming's age. But he doesn't believe Ming is unique. "There are no doubt older clams in the ocean, even older ocean quahogs," Austad explains. "Considering that there are [likely] many millions of them alive right now, it would be remarkable if we [had] happened by chance to catch the oldest one. There are likely other bivalve species, yet to be discovered, that routinely live to even older ages."

Austad is trying to determine how the ocean quahog can live for so long. He has found that ocean quahogs "have a remarkable ability to prevent some common problems of aging. One of these is the ability to resist proteins inside the cells from clumping together, gumming up the cells' normal processes."

Austad explains, "Such clumps are involved in Alzheimer's and Parkinson's disease [which generally affect older people] and some muscle diseases, and [we] suspect they are involved in many problems of aging. The fluids from ocean quahogs even prevent clumping in the protein that we think causes Alzheimer's disease." Austad concluded, "There is no doubt more to their exceptional longevity, but this is what we know now."

Professor Steven N. Austad displays two ocean quahogs in his laboratory at the University of Alabama in Birmingham. The oldest quahog ever found was born in 1499. Austad believes that even older quahogs are alive in the world's oceans.

The results were incredible. The second-largest shark in the study was just over 16 feet (4.9 m) long and was found to be at least 260 years old and possibly up to 410 years old. The largest shark was close to 16.5 feet (5 m) long and was at least 272 years old and possibly up to 512 years old. Even the low ends of the age ranges suggested that the Greenland shark was the longest-lived vertebrate (animal with a backbone) in the world.

Nielsen and his team estimate that Greenland sharks do not reproduce until they are at least 130 years old. This fact puts the shark in greater danger of extinction than fish that reproduce when they are much younger. Here's why: Humans hunt sharks commercially. For several hundred years, commercial fisheries heavily targeted Greenland sharks for the oil in their livers. The oil was burned in lamps and used to lubricate machines, just like whale oil. Sales of shark liver oil dropped off in the mid-twentieth century, but by then, Greenland shark populations were low. In the twenty-first century, commercial fishing operations commonly net Greenland sharks as bycatch (accidental captures) when they are fishing for halibut and other kinds of edible fish. And some Icelandic fishers deliberately target Greenland sharks for their meat. So humans are still catching and killing many Greenland sharks, including those that are younger than 130 years—too young to reproduce. And if humans kill too many Greenland sharks before they can reproduce, the population of the species will decline. The species could even die out altogether.

Nielsen, who published his findings in August 2016, wants to know more about the Greenland shark's biology and behavior. His PhD project also includes data on how Greenland sharks reproduce and where and when they migrate. He believes that knowing more about how Greenland sharks live, including how long they live, can help us protect these centuries-old creatures.

CHAPTER 3

A HYDRA AND A JELLYFISH: NEAR IMMORTALS

Ponds are filled with familiar creatures: frogs, snails, turtles, ducks, and fish. Ponds don't have the drama of the Arctic Ocean, with its crashing ice floes and incredibly old creatures like the Greenland shark. But if you think ponds aren't mysterious, you just haven't looked closely enough.

Living in ponds are some of the most fascinating creatures of all—and they break the rules for aging. These distant relatives of jellyfish live in freshwater ponds, rivers, and lakes around the world. They are hydras—small, tentacled animals that have some amazing abilities.

THE TINY HYDRA

Look at underwater plants, twigs, or rocks in a pond, and a hydra will probably be on one of them. Measuring less than

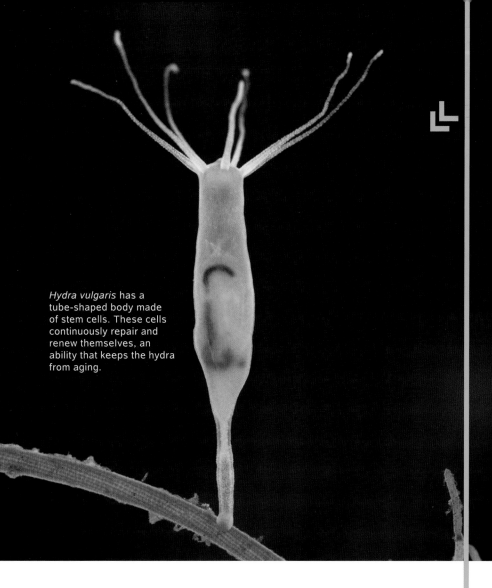

Hydra vulgaris has a tube-shaped body made of stem cells. These cells continuously repair and renew themselves, an ability that keeps the hydra from aging.

1 inch (2.5 cm) long, the hydra is a simple tube without internal body organs. At one end is a sticky disk: its foot. At the other end is its head: a mouth surrounded by a ring of up to twelve tentacles. At first glance, the hydra seems pretty harmless. But it's a deadly killer! Packed with stinging cells, the hydra's waving tentacles capture prey such as small shrimp and fleas and inject paralyzing toxins into them. The hydra pulls its helpless victims into its tube-shaped body to digest.

BIOLOGICAL BLUEPRINT: *HYDRA VULGARIS*

Common name: white hydra

Scientific name: *Hydra vulgaris*

Habitat: freshwater ponds, rivers, and lakes around the world (except Antarctica)

Diet: carnivorous, eating small freshwater animals such as crustaceans, worms, and insect larvae

Length: less than 1 inch (2.5 cm)

Life span: potentially immortal—if living in ideal conditions without predators, such as in a laboratory

Curious adaptation: A hydra does not have a permanent mouth or anal opening like most animals. When it eats, the cells around its mouth stretch apart to create an opening. Once food is inside the hydra's body, the cells relax and the tissue around the mouth seals up again. After the food is digested, the mouth rips open again and the hydra expels any unused food as waste. Then the mouth seals shut again until the hydra's next meal.

The hydra has a unique way of moving from one spot to another. It does a kind of somersault. It bends its body forward, grabs a nearby plant with its tentacles, and then releases its foot from the plant or rock where it's been stationed. The foot swings overhead and attaches itself to a new spot.

Growing quickly, the hydra reaches sexual maturity fast. Just five to ten days after it is born, it can start to reproduce. Most animals reproduce by mating with a species member of the opposite sex. But many kinds of hydras reproduce asexually, without mating. Instead, they grow several mini-hydra buds off the sides of their bodies. The buds detach from the adults after a few days and become independent baby hydras.

This small animal may be easy to miss, but starting in the early eighteenth century, it caught the attention of scientists. One of the first people to study hydras was Swiss naturalist Abraham Trembley, who noticed them in a pond in 1740. He cut a hydra in half to see what would happen. Trembley expected it to die, but to his surprise, the halves grew into two complete hydras. Even smaller cut pieces of hydras regenerated into whole hydras. At that time, biologists knew that some plants have the ability to regenerate from cut pieces and that some animals regrow amputated limbs. But complete regeneration as Trembley observed in hydras had never been observed before in animals. Biologists later found that even a tiny fragment of a hydra's body tissue will grow into a new hydra.

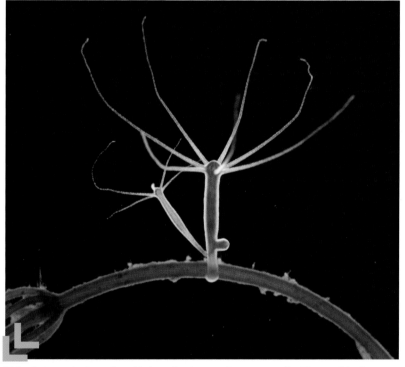

This photograph shows how *Hydra vulgaris* reproduces asexually. The small hydra on the left has budded from the larger parent hydra. After most animals reproduce, they age and then die. But hydras reproduce again and again, and they don't appear to age.

A CLAIM WITHOUT DATA

In the twentieth century, other biologists studied the hydra and noticed another curious thing. Most creatures the size of hydras die days or weeks after they reproduce. But *Hydra vulgaris*, one of the species of the genus *Hydra*, did not seem to age at all. Hydras of this species didn't stop reproducing, and their bodies didn't deteriorate over time. In 1953 Belgian researcher Paul Brien claimed that hydras were immortal. Brien believed that although they could die of diseases, they were also capable of living forever. This claim inspired another scientist to try to prove Brien wrong.

That scientist was evolutionary biologist Daniel Martinez, who became interested in aging as a PhD student at Stony Brook University in New York in the early 1990s. At that time, Martinez and the rest of the scientific community believed that all animals aged—that none could escape aging and death. Biologists thought that "aging was something that . . . made sense. There were models, mathematical models, that showed why we should age," Martinez explains. So a claim of hydra immortality *had* to be wrong.

Martinez says, "It was a claim, but there was no data. There were just anecdotes, people saying, 'Oh I have a hydra [that's lived] for four years,' but nobody had done the experiments." Martinez started his experiments in his last two years of graduate school. He was going to prove that the hydra ages and dies, just like any other animal on Earth.

NEVER-ENDING EXPERIMENTS

Martinez collected samples of *Hydra vulgaris* from a pond in Long Island, New York. He took them back to the lab, gave them the best possible living conditions—clean water and fresh food—to keep them safe from disease and injury, and began watching the individuals. And he watched some more. He fed them tiny, newly hatched brine shrimp, changed their water regularly, and continued watching.

EVOLUTION: HOW LIFE DEVELOPED ON EARTH

The theory of evolution describes how the many forms of life developed on Earth. All Earth's organisms descended from an ancient common ancestor. Over millions of years, these life-forms changed and developed in response to environmental conditions. For example, some creatures developed beaks to help them break open seeds. Others developed fins and smooth skin to swim efficiently through water. Some plants developed large, brightly colored flowers to attract butterflies and birds. These animals frequently transfer pollen (male sex cells) from one part of a flower to another, helping plants reproduce. Other plants developed sensitive leaves to trap insects, which the plants then digest for nutrients.

Each living thing passes on traits to its offspring by passing along its genes. Certain traits, such as green coloring or the ability to fly, might help a living thing survive longer than creatures that don't have these traits. And if it survives long enough to reproduce, it will pass on the helpful traits to its offspring. But if an organism does not have traits that help it survive, it might die before it is mature enough to reproduce. If enough of its kind die without reproducing, the species might become extinct. Meanwhile, the species that has passed on its survival abilities to its offspring will thrive. Organisms that best adapt to their environments thrive and reproduce, while those that are less well suited die out. This is called natural selection.

Organisms evolve over many generations, developing traits that assist in survival. The Venus flytrap developed sensitive leaves, which snap shut to trap insects. The plant then digests them.

EVOLUTIONARY BIOLOGIST DANIEL MARTINEZ: EXPLORING FOR HYDRA

Growing up in Argentina, Daniel Martinez didn't want to be a biologist. He wanted to be an explorer and go backpacking, ride a motorcycle, and see the world. But he felt that being an explorer wasn't practical, so he went to college in Argentina, where he studied marine biology. Martinez then went to Stony Brook University in New York to study for his PhD. At Stony Brook, he became more and more interested in evolution. Along with evolution, Martinez also became interested in aging, which brought him to the hydra.

Martinez collects hydras from a river in eastern California.

Martinez is on a mission to clear up whether hydras from different parts of the globe are the same or different species. Hydras have few distinguishing physical features, so it is very difficult to tell one species from another. In the twentieth century, biologists looked for tiny differences in the organization of hydras' body parts. From these observations, they categorized hydras into eighty different species. By the 1980s, biologists had a new technology to work with—genetics. The cells of all living things contain entwined strands of deoxyribonucleic acid (DNA). DNA holds the instructions for how each living thing will grow, reproduce, and function. Segments of DNA are called genes. To study plant's or animal's DNA, biologists look inside cells using high-powered microscopes and other machines.

Martinez travels the world to find hydras for his research. He has collected hydras on every continent except Antarctica, where they do not live. He takes them back to his lab in California and tests their DNA. From similarities and differences in the DNA, he has identified eight—not eighty—hydra species.

Martinez will continue to document the types of hydras he finds, even after he is done with his aging research. "That's something that interests me—to see if there are new hydras in the world somewhere. So I get to go to beautiful places and try to find hydras," Martinez says. It turns out he is an explorer after all—he just arrived there through studying hydras.

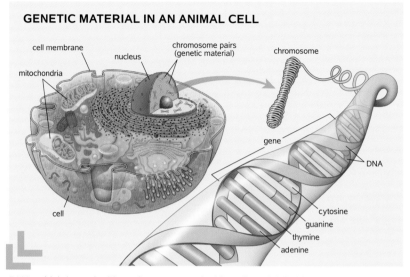

GENETIC MATERIAL IN AN ANIMAL CELL

cell membrane

mitochondria

nucleus

chromosome pairs
(genetic material)

chromosome

gene

DNA

cell

cytosine

guanine

thymine

adenine

DNA, which is packed into chromosomes inside cell nuclei, holds instructions for how living things behave, grow, and reproduce. DNA is made of the chemical compounds guanine, cytosine, adenine, and thymine. Specific segments of DNA are called genes.

It was tedious, time-consuming work. Two years later, "I graduated and I finished my dissertation and there were very few [hydra] deaths. Most of the animals I studied were still there." Meanwhile, Martinez had a new research post across the country, at the University of California (UC)–Irvine. He had to move, but what would he do with the hydras? They had already lived a couple of years, which was extraordinary for creatures so small. Usually creatures the size of hydras live only a few days or weeks. Martinez decided, "Okay I am going to continue this experiment—this is really weird." So he put the hydras in a cooler and took them with him on the drive to California.

In Irvine the hydras continued living another two years, making them at least four years old. By then Martinez was convinced that hydras were unique animals. In 1998 he published a paper stating that *Hydra vulgaris* does not seem to age. Then he moved on to other research. But other scholars noticed his paper, and in 2005, the Max

ROAD TRIPPING WITH HYDRAS

Daniel Martinez took his hydras with him when he moved from New York to California. His brother helped him make the two-week drive in a rented U-Haul truck. It had a broken air conditioner, though, making it difficult to keep the hydras at just the right temperature, about 64°F to 70°F (18°C to 21°C), while driving through the hot US Southwest. So Martinez kept the hydras in a cooler with ice. Caring for them on the road trip was a lot of work. He had to feed them, keep their water clean, and keep enough ice in the cooler.

The brothers did a little sightseeing along the way. They stopped at national parks, and "I remember feeding the hydra on a picnic table in Zion [National Park] in Utah," Martinez says. "And in order to feed them you had to have brine shrimp that you just hatched. They had to be fresh brine shrimp. So I had to carry the eggs, and I hatched the brine shrimp." Shrimp eggs need to be in bubbling water to hatch, but Martinez didn't have to worry about making bubbles. The truck's movement kept the shrimp's water moving and bubbling, so the eggs readily hatched. Despite the difficult ride, the hydra survived the trip to California, and the aging experiment continued.

Planck Institute for Demographic Research in Rostock, Germany, proposed collaborating with him on a large-scale hydra study. Martinez agreed, and after eight years observing hydras in that study, the researchers came up with the same conclusion. In 2015 they published a paper saying that hydras do not age. And if they don't age, Brien must have been right. They must be immortal.

By 2017 Martinez's hydras were eleven years old and they showed no signs of aging. Why? Martinez and his colleagues think they have discovered the answer. Most of *Hydra vulgaris*'s body is made from stem cells, a kind of cell found in all multicellular animals. Animals start out from a single cell, a fertilized egg. The egg begins dividing, resulting in more cells. These are stem cells. They are undifferentiated, or able to turn into any kind of cell for any part of the animal's body. As the animal's cells continue to divide and multiply, they begin to differentiate, or specialize, for certain areas of the body. Some become muscle or nerve cells. Others change into gland cells and cells used in other body parts.

In *Hydra vulgaris*, however, the stem cells of its tube-shaped body don't turn into specialized cells. When they divide, they simply remain stem cells. And like stem cells in general, they can repair and replace damaged tissue. That's how *Hydra vulgaris* regenerates its own damaged body parts. The stem cells also allow *Hydra vulgaris* to grow baby hydra buds from its body. So the stem cells continually give the creature a new body, preventing it from aging and dying. The hydra contradicts what Martinez believed at the beginning of his career—that everything ages. Now Martinez says, "Hydras seem to be an exception."

A MOST UNUSUAL JELLYFISH

In the Mediterranean Sea lives a distant relative of the hydra that escapes death in a very different way. About as wide as a person's pinkie finger, its translucent umbrella-shaped body has a glowing red stomach and up to ninety thin, white waving tentacles. It is *Turritopsis dohrnii*, a unique kind of jellyfish.

Many marine animals, including jellyfish, go through a metamorphosis during their life cycle, changing from one form to another. The *Turritopsis dohrnii* life cycle begins with sexual reproduction. Males produce sperm and release them onto eggs that females have deposited in the water. The sperm fertilizes the eggs, which turn into planulae. These organisms look like small balls with hairlike projections. Planulae fall to the seafloor, where they grow into a colony of polyps (tubelike creatures with tentacles). Then the polyps grow buds that detach to become young medusae, or independent jellyfish. These young jellyfish grow into adult jellyfish, which can reproduce sexually.

After an adult jellyfish reproduces sexually, it soon dies. But under certain circumstances, *Turritopsis dohrnii* can extend its life in an extraordinary way. If a medusa is injured or stressed—by lack of food,

BIOLOGICAL BLUEPRINT: *TURRITOPSIS DOHRNII*

Common name: immortal jellyfish

Scientific name: *Turritopsis dohrnii*

Habitat: originally from the Ligurian Sea (an arm of the Mediterranean Sea)

Diet: carnivorous, eating plankton, fish eggs, and small mollusks

Length: 0.2 inches (4.5 mm) tall and wide

Life span: potentially immortal, if repeatedly stressed

Curious adaptation: When stressed or damaged, these jellyfish can transform into polyps, which produce new jellyfish.

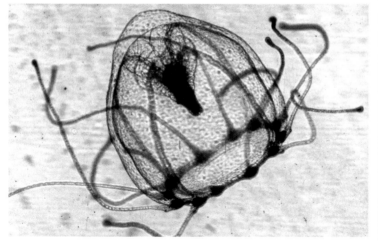

If an adult *Turritopsis dohrnii* (*above*) is stressed or injured, it can return to the polyp stage of its life cycle and release new medusae.

changes in water salinity (saltiness), or a disease or injury—*Turritopsis dohrnii* can reverse its life cycle. It goes back in time to its earlier polyp life stage. Then it begins budding again, producing new medusae. If it is stressed again, the jellyfish could potentially live forever in this cycle, going back and forth between medusa and polyp stages. It's a bit like

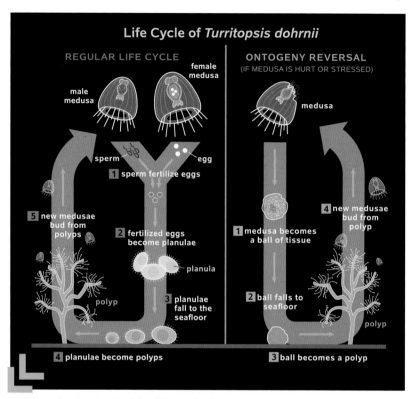

Life Cycle of *Turritopsis dohrnii*

REGULAR LIFE CYCLE

female medusa

male medusa

sperm — egg

1 sperm fertilize eggs

5 new medusae bud from polyps

2 fertilized eggs become planulae

planula

polyp

3 planulae fall to the seafloor

4 planulae become polyps

ONTOGENY REVERSAL
(IF MEDUSA IS HURT OR STRESSED)

medusa

4 new medusae bud from polyp

1 medusa becomes a ball of tissue

2 ball falls to seafloor

polyp

3 ball becomes a polyp

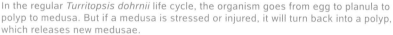

In the regular *Turritopsis dohrnii* life cycle, the organism goes from egg to planula to polyp to medusa. But if a medusa is stressed or injured, it will turn back into a polyp, which releases new medusae.

a butterfly (the jellyfish) turning back into a caterpillar (the polyp) to become a butterfly again, indefinitely. Some researchers call *Turritopsis dohrnii* the immortal jellyfish, but that animal doesn't live forever, like the hydra. Instead, the adult jellyfish's cells reorganize themselves into a polyp, which then produces brand-new jellyfish.

This process, called ontogeny reversal, was discovered in the 1980s by accident during a study headed by Ferdinando Boero, a zoology professor at the University of Salento in Lecce, Italy. Boero undertook the study, along with his students Christian Sommer and Giorgio Bavestrello, to learn more about the jellyfish life cycle.

THE FORGOTTEN MEDUSAE

To carry out the study, Sommer and Bavestrello collected jellyfish polyps in the Ligurian Sea off the coast of Portofino, Italy. They collected many different kinds of polyps, including some they thought were *Turritopsis nutricula*. (They later learned that the species was *Turritopsis dohrnii*.) They brought the polyps to the lab, placed them in small glass bowls called rearing jars, and cared for them until they released tiny medusae. Then the students forgot to check on the medusae until two days later.

When they went back to the forgotten medusae, "instead of medusa corpses, they found little polyps," Boero explains. "Those polyps came from the medusae, not from planulas. And that was strange."

The team investigated further. They observed that stressed young medusae transformed into balls of tissue, which fell to the bottom of the rearing jars. The balls of tissue then grew into new polyps, which released medusae. So these new jellyfish were created outside the creature's normal life cycle.

CHANGING CELLS

Sommer and Bavestrello presented their discovery at a meeting of the Hydrozoan Society in Blanes, Spain, in 1991. Among the many attendees were Boero and Volker Schmid, a developmental biologist from the Zoological Institute at the University of Basel in Switzerland.

Schmid had studied a similar kind of life stage reversal in medusa buds that were still attached to polyps. He didn't believe it was possible for free-floating medusae to become polyps again though. So Boero decided to demonstrate for him. He remembered, "I went in the water and found *Turritopsis*. I brought it back to the laboratory. It [released] medusae. So we obtained newly liberated medusae. Volker Schmid stressed them with a little cut and we waited. They all transformed into polyps, in a few hours. Volker was *very* surprised."

Schmid and another of Boero's students, Stefano Piraino, then studied the cells of four hundred medusae. They published a paper on

IMMORTAL JELLYFISH MAN

Japanese biologist Shin Kubota spent several long periods in Lecce, Italy, in Ferdinando Boero's lab, where he became familiar with *Turritopsis dohrnii*. Then he started to work with the species at his own lab at Kyoto University in Japan. He grows the jellyfish, stresses them, and then watches them transform into polyps. Kubota says, "Once we determine how the jellyfish rejuvenates itself, we should achieve very great things." He thinks researchers might use this knowledge to halt human aging.

You can watch Mr. Immortal Jellyfish Man (Shin Kubota) on YouTube, where he also explains how *Turritopsis dohrnii* cheats death.

Kubota has a fun alter ego: Mr. Immortal Jellyfish Man. He even wears a Mr. Immortal Jellyfish Man costume—a red cap with tentacles and a white lab coat. A big karaoke fan, Kubota loves to sing, and he has written many songs about *Turritopsis dohrnii*. Kubota performs in karaoke bars and on Japanese TV wearing his Immortal Jellyfish Man outfit.

their findings in 1996. They found that the key to *Turritopsis dohrnii*'s regenerative ability comes from their cells. "Usually, when cells are differentiated, their destiny is written. They are not able to shift to other cell types," Boero explains. This is not the case with *Turritopsis dohrnii*. When stressed, it goes through transdifferentiation. Its life cycle reversal can happen because its specialized cells can change into other specialized cells. This allows the jellyfish to transform from a medusa into a polyp.

Medical researchers are especially interested in knowing more about transdifferentiation, as it has potential medical uses for humans. For instance, perhaps transdifferentiation could turn cancerous human cells into healthy cells. Before that can happen, researchers must learn more about *Turritopsis dohrnii*'s unusual survival skill.

CHAPTER 4
GLASS SPONGE REEFS AND STROMATOLITES: BACK FROM THE DEAD

Deep underwater in some oceans, attached to the seafloor, are what look like groups of rocks or oddly shaped, unmoving plants. But they're actually animals. With their long, thin stalks, some look like delicate spires. Others are more robust, with thicker cup-shaped or tube-shaped bodies. They don't move, and they can't see or feel, but they breathe, eat, and grow. The animals are glass sponges, primitive sea creatures that filter food through thousands of tiny holes in their bodies. Glass sponges belong to an ancient animal group that first lived on Earth more than eight hundred million years ago. As water flows through them, the sponges trap oxygen, a mineral called silicon dioxide (or silica), and small particles of dead animals and plants. These substances give the sponges everything they need to survive.

Glass sponges use silica—found in sand (which humans melt

Glass sponges have been on Earth for two hundred million years. These delicate organisms with glass-like skeletons can easily shatter, yet they have incredibly long life spans.

to make glass)—to build their skeletons. The silica forms needlelike, translucent spicules that reach upward through the seawater. In some glass sponge skeletons, the spicules crisscross to form a tight grid pattern. Other sponges have loose spicule skeletons, held together by thin layers of soft tissue. Hidden away at the bottom of the sea, sponges probably reach very old ages—living perhaps hundreds of years.

Glass sponges were first discovered in the 1870s during the four-year, British-led Challenger Expedition, the world's first scientific oceanographic study. From aboard the steamship HMS *Challenger*, outfitted with scientific equipment and a pair of laboratories, a team of scientists gathered data about the ocean floor. They used different instruments to take water temperature readings, chart the weather, and make other measurements. They also lowered weighted nets to dredge the seabed. They hauled up the nets and studied and preserved the many animals and plants captured in them. Among those animals were glass sponges, which the expedition recorded in detail. As later marine biologists studied glass sponges further, they discovered just how remarkable these creatures are.

LIVING FOSSILS

About 200 million years ago, enormous glass sponge reefs—groups of glass sponges growing together—formed in an ancient ocean called the Tethys Sea, which once covered parts of modern-day Europe. As Earth changed over millions of years, the sea grew smaller. Parts of Europe once covered by the Tethys Sea still hold the remains of glass sponge reefs. The reefs have fossilized, or turned into stone. The fossilized reefs are found across Europe in rocky outcrops from Spain and southern France to Poland and Romania. The ancient reefs once covered 4,350 miles (7,000 km) of the Tethys seafloor, where they flourished for 180 million years. Through much of the twentieth century, geologists and other scientists believed that the reefs had gone extinct about 40 million years ago. But in 1987, geologists discovered that living glass sponge reefs still exist on Earth.

During a survey in the early 1980s, geologists with the Geological Survey of Canada, a government organization, were mapping the seafloor of Hecate Strait, a wide waterway off the western coast of British Columbia, Canada. Using a technology called sonar, the geologists sent sound waves to the seafloor. The waves hit the floor and bounced back. By analyzing the returning sound waves, the researchers could determine the depth and contours of the ocean floor. They believed the seafloor in that area was quite flat, but the sonar data showed something very different—huge, tall mounds spread over much of the area. In 1987, using a remote-controlled camera, the geologists discovered that the mounds were living glass sponge reefs.

Many were stunned by this discovery—glass sponge reefs weren't extinct after all! Manfred Krautter of the University of Stuttgart in Germany, an expert on fossilized glass sponge reefs in Europe, likened the Canadian discovery to finding a "living herd of dinosaurs." The reefs cover 386 square miles (1,000 sq. km) and reach more than 60 feet (19 m) high, almost the height of a six-story building. Since that 1987 discovery, researchers have found ten smaller reefs off the Canadian coast. And in 2007, University of Washington marine geologist Paul Johnson discovered a glass sponge reef off the coast of Washington State.

Marine biologists believe the reefs of the Pacific Northwest began forming around nine thousand years ago. After their discovery, researchers found that three main kinds of glass sponges interlock to make the "bones" of these reefs. These are the finger goblet sponge (*Heterochone calyx*), the cloud sponge (*Aphrocallistes vastus*), and *Farrea occa* (a sponge with no common name). The reefs are a rich habitat for many other sea creatures, such as octopuses, crabs, shrimps, and rockfish.

SHATTERED GLASS: DAMAGE TO THE REEFS

The discovery that glass sponge reefs are not extinct was thrilling news. Yet human activities in the twenty-first century may actually be causing them to die out for real. Fishing crews have dropped and dragged nets, traps, boat cables, and anchors over the sponge reefs off the western coast of Canada. This equipment has broken glass sponge skeletons, which are fragile and meringue-like, and killed many sponges in the reefs. Fishing and other water-based industry also stir up large amounts of sediment from the seafloor, blocking the holes through which sponges absorb the nutrients and oxygen they need to survive. Nearly half of Canada's glass sponge reefs may have died because of such harmful activity.

To save the delicate structures, the Canadian government banned bottom-contact fishing within 0.6 miles (1 km) of the glass sponge reefs in Hecate Strait and Queen Charlotte Sound. Such laws will keep reefs in Canadian waters safe in the short term. However, climate change is warming ocean temperatures, which may harm the biological systems that sponges use to draw nutrients into their bodies. Warm water also holds less oxygen than cold water, so as waters

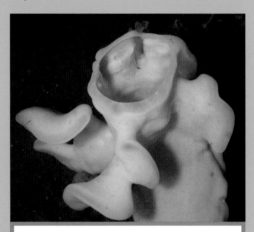

An individual glass sponge in a Canadian reef. Glass sponges are fragile. Fishing nets and boat cables can easily break them. Global climate change is also affecting the temperature and chemistry of ocean water, posing additional threats to glass sponges.

warm, oxygen levels fall. If warming continues, glass sponges might not have enough oxygen to survive. Marine biologists are closely watching glass sponge reefs to learn more about the long-term impact of climate change on these fragile life-forms and to take steps to protect them.

Remotely operated vehicles (ROVs) can navigate deep underwater to take images, gather data, and map the ocean floor. Sally Leys and her team use ROVs to study glass sponge reefs.

The reefs also are a nursery for very young creatures, which can hide from predators and grow inside their crevices.

The Pacific Northwest also has communities of individual glass sponges, which are not part of reefs. In the early 1990s, University of Alberta professor and glass sponge researcher Sally Leys set out to find the age of some of these individuals. She focused on twenty-one glass sponges belonging to the species *Rhabdocalyptus dawsoni* in Saanich Inlet, a steep-walled waterway on the coast of Vancouver Island, at the northwestern tip of Washington State. Leys photographed the sponges every few months for three years. She was looking for yearly and seasonal growth patterns, and she found that the sponges grew less than 1 inch (2 cm) each year. The average-size sponge was just under 1 foot (3 m) tall, but some of the largest were more than 3.3 feet (1 m) tall.

ELECTRICAL SIGNALS

Many animals, including humans, have nervous systems to transmit information throughout the body. A nervous system allows an animal to sense what's happening in the world around it and to adjust to changes in its environment. In humans and other animals, the nervous system consists of nerve cells, a spinal cord, and a brain. The nervous system operates by sending electrical signals from one part of the body to another. The nervous system gives humans the ability to think, feel, and react to the outside world. The nervous system also controls many human body processes, such as breathing and heartbeat.

A glass sponge doesn't have a brain, nerves, or a spine, so it can't sense or respond to its environment the same way other animals do. But in 1997, Sally Leys and George Mackie of the University of Victoria in British Columbia discovered something very unexpected about the sponges. Leys says, "The coolest thing about glass sponges is that they . . . can send electrical signals [from one part of the body to another] just as in animals with nervous systems."

Leys explains that glass sponges use these electrical signals to prevent sediment from clogging their bodies. They send the signals to stop flagella, threadlike structures in their tissues, from moving and pulling sediment-filled water into their bodies. This keeps sediment from entering the holes in their tissue that normally absorb nutrients. Otherwise, if the holes were to clog, a sponge could die.

Leys wonders, "Why does this group of sponges—alone among all sponges—have an electrical conduction system?" Leys thinks that glass sponges may have developed the electrical signals in response to the low amounts of food in their deep-sea habitat. They needed a way to ensure a steady food supply, and their bodies evolved an electrical system to help protect this supply. Through her research, Leys hopes to find out whether this is true.

Based on that growth rate, Leys calculated that the average sponge in her study was "about 35 years old, while a meter-long [3.3-foot] sponge was about 200 to 250 years old."

Dating an entire glass sponge reef is more difficult. That's because reefs form when older sponges die and younger sponges grow on top of them. New sponges keep growing and connecting with one another to make a continuous living structure. So to date a reef's age accurately, marine biologists need to find a sponge that has grown from the reef's base. Distinguishing between the skeletons of living sponges and dead sponges in a reef can be difficult, but Leys believes the larger sponges in the reefs may be about four hundred years old.

PORTALS TO THE PAST

A different kind of living fossil thrives in shallow ocean waters, mostly in the Bahamas (islands in the Atlantic Ocean near Florida) and in Shark Bay on Australia's western coast. Known as stromatolites, these rounded rock formations rise above the water in groups that look a bit like stepping-stones. Parts of them are rocks, but their topmost layers are alive. They contain microscopic, single-celled organisms called cyanobacteria. They live in communities of millions of organisms.

Earth formed about 4.6 billion years ago. When the planet was young, stromatolites dominated the world's oceans.

"THERE IS A NEVER-ENDING QUEST TO FIND OLDER AND OLDER EVIDENCE OF THE FIRST FORMS OF LIFE ON EARTH."

—MARINE GEOSCIENTIST PAMELA REID

Stromatolites were among the first living things on Earth and have survived into the twenty-first century. These stromatolites in the Bahamas might look like rock formations, but their top layers hold living cyanobacteria.

Earth's atmosphere had very little oxygen then, but the cyanobacteria in stromatolites started changing the atmosphere. That's because cyanobacteria undergo photosynthesis. They use the energy of sunlight filtering into the water, in combination with carbon dioxide and water, to make sugar, the fuel they need to grow and carry out life processes. (Algae, green plants, and some other bacteria rely on photosynthesis too.) As cyanobacteria take in carbon dioxide, they release oxygen.

When cyanobacteria in stromatolites released oxygen during photosynthesis billions of years ago, they helped oxygenate Earth's atmosphere. Over time, the extra oxygen in the atmosphere enabled other life-forms to develop.

Geologists and other scientists study fossilized stromatolites to learn about early Earth. To date these ancient fossils, scientists measure levels of potassium in the rock. Potassium, a metallic element, begins to decay after a rock forms, and the rate of decay is known and constant. So the amount of potassium in a rock tells geologists how long a rock has been decaying—and thus the rock's age. Pamela Reid, a marine geoscientist at the University of Miami in Florida, says that researchers are finding older and older stromatolites. "[At one point], the oldest documented [fossilized] stromatolites were 3.5 billion years. New discoveries pushed this age to 3.7 billion years, and the latest reports [from 2017] go back to 4.2 billion years," Reid says. "There is a never-ending quest to find older and older evidence of the first forms of life on Earth." Stromatolites may be one of them.

STUDYING LIVING STROMATOLITES

Earth scientists say that most stromatolites disappeared about six hundred million years ago. That's when large communities of seaweed first developed. Growing in the water above stromatolites, the seaweed blocked and used for themselves the sunlight that the stromatolites' cyanobacteria need for photosynthesis.

"IT IS INSPIRING TO WORK IN AN ECOSYSTEM THAT HAS PERSISTED ON EARTH FOR OVER 3 BILLION YEARS."

—MARINE GEOSCIENTIST PAMELA REID

PAMELA REID: FIELDWORK WITH STROMATOLITES

Many biologists spend most of their time in laboratories, analyzing organisms' molecules under microscopes. Marine geoscientist Pamela Reid of the University of Miami in Florida believes there's much to be learned from "old-fashioned fieldwork. Nothing beats detailed field observations," she says.

From a small research station in the Bahamas, Reid and her team monitored the daily and weekly growth patterns of stromatolites from 2003 to 2008. Their work revealed important information that only careful on-site observation could provide. For example, Reid and her team found that on average stromatolites in the Bahamas grow only about 0.04 inches (1 mm) per year. But sometimes they grow "a few centimeters in a few months." Reid explains that because of shifting sands, "stromatolite growth is sporadic. . . . New sediment can be eroded, or the stromatolites may become buried and [stop growing] for months." She points out that "the stromatolite beach we monitored was extremely dynamic, with sand shifting and [sometimes] burying and unburying stromatolites by as much as a meter [3.3 feet] overnight."

Pamela Reid, equipped with scuba gear, heads out to study stromatolites off the beach at Little Darby Island in the Bahamas.

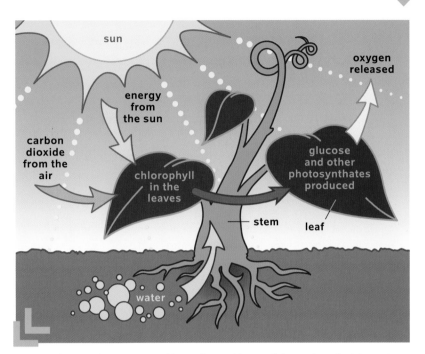

Plants, algae, and some types of bacteria combine sunlight, carbon dioxide, and water to make food. During this process, called photosynthesis, oxygen is released into the air. Billions of years ago, the cyanobacteria on stromatolites put large amounts of oxygen into the atmosphere via photosynthesis.

But in the twenty-first century, millions of years later, some stromatolites still survive. A team led by geologist Brian W. Logan of the University of Western Australia in Perth first discovered living stromatolites in 1956 while exploring Shark Bay. When the tide went out in Hamelin Pool, part of the bay with high salinity, the team was amazed by what they saw. Stony structures standing 3.3 to 6.6 feet (1 to 2 m) tall covered the shoreline. On the tops were sticky mats of cyanobacteria. The geologists realized they were not fossilized stromatolites—they were alive!

Observing the living stromatolites, the geologists found out how stromatolites grow. As ocean currents shift back and forth, sediment and minerals become trapped in the slimy, sticky layer made by the cyanobacteria. The sediment and minerals pile up in layers and harden over time, creating domelike forms that rise higher and higher from the floor of the ocean. As each layer forms, the cyanobacteria migrate up from below to cover the top layer.

Since the 1956 discovery, more living stromatolites have been discovered around the world. They live in areas where other life-forms do not compete with them for sunlight. Some stromatolites thrive in harsh conditions that are inhospitable to most plants and animals. In Shark Bay, the water is too salty for most life, but cyanobacteria thrive there. Some conditions are right for stromatolites but not for organisms that would block their sunlight. In the Bahamas, for instance, fast-moving tides generate sand waves, which periodically bury the stromatolites. The sand keeps seaweeds and corals from growing above the stromatolites. Without that competition for sunlight, the cyanobacteria flourish and the stromatolites continue to grow.

Reid studies living stromatolites in Shark Bay and the Bahamas. They are about one thousand to three thousand years old, she says.

Microscopic cyanobacteria, which form a sticky layer at the top of stromatolites, use sunlight filtering through the water to make energy via photosynthesis. To study stromatolites, researchers often dive to the seafloor.

Reid is working to figure out growth models for stromatolites in the Shark Bay system. She says, "It is inspiring to work in an ecosystem that has persisted on Earth for over 3 billion years."

CHAPTER 5

TUATARA:
REPTILE RELICS

With rising cliffs covered in lush vegetation, a group of Pacific islands is home to animals whose ancestors lived, more than two hundred million years ago, long before the age of dinosaurs. Together the islands make up New Zealand. Because the vast Pacific Ocean surrounds the islands, the animals of New Zealand evolved in isolation for millions of years. No large land mammals ever developed on the islands. Without mammals to prey on them, smaller creatures thrived there.

One of these creatures is the last surviving member of the reptilian order of Rhynchocephalia, a once diverse group of reptiles that thrived for tens of millions of years. Some biologists call this animal a living fossil because of its connection to an otherwise extinct order of animals. This small reptile is the tuatara. Just one tuatara species exists, and it is found only in New Zealand.

As a species, the tuatara is extremely long-lived, having emerged on Earth more than two hundred million years ago.

THE SPINY-BACKED REPTILE

With its green, wrinkled skin and clawed feet, the 2-foot-long (0.6 m) tuatara looks like a miniature dinosaur. Along its head and spine are the spikes that give this reptile its name. *Tuatara* means "spiny back" in the language of the Maori, the indigenous people of New Zealand. The spikes are made of soft tissue and are not sharp enough to harm enemies. But when a male tuatara wants to attract a female or frighten other animals away from his territory, he makes the spikes stick straight up.

Growing atop the tuatara's head is a third, or parietal, eye. The eye can be seen on the head of a young tuatara, but as the reptile matures, pigmented, or colored, scales grow over the eye. The eye has a retina, lens, and nerve endings just like a regular eye. These structures allow ordinary eyes to gather light and transmit visual information to the brain. The parietal eye cannot process images as an ordinary eye can, but it is sensitive to light. Herpetologists (scientists who study reptiles) think the third eye may help this cold-blooded creature adjust its body temperature when it shifts from hot sun to cool shade and back again. Tuatara may also use this light-sensitive eye as a kind of compass. They can move toward or away from the light to find their way through unfamiliar territory. Some Maori tribes believe this eye allows the tuatara to see into the spirit world. They regard tuatara as the *kaitiaki* (guardians) of what they call the stream of knowledge.

Without large mammals to prey on them, tuatara flourished on New Zealand's two main islands for millions of years. Then, around the thirteenth century, humans from other South Pacific islands arrived in New Zealand by boat. Later, European explorers and settlers came to New Zealand. The newcomers brought mammals, such as dogs, cats, rats, and pigs. These animals preyed on tuatara, eating their eggs and young. Over time, rats and other predators killed off tuatara on New Zealand's two main islands.

In the twenty-first century, these reptiles survive only on about thirty small islands off New Zealand's two main islands. These islands

THE ENDANGERED KAKAPO

New Zealand is home to another longevity master, the kakapo. It is the heaviest parrot in the world, it can't fly (unlike all other parrots), and it moves around only at night. Some New Zealanders say that it smells like peaches.

Parrots are long-lived birds. Many live almost as long as people do. But the kakapo has many parrots beat in the longevity game. Most kakapos reach the ripe old age of fifty-eight, but some have lived to be ninety.

Like the tuatara, the kakapo thrived before people brought mammals to New Zealand. Predators such as rats and cats nearly wiped out the population. In the late twentieth century, New Zealand conservation groups relocated a handful of surviving kakapos to island sanctuaries, away from predators. By 2017 the kakapo population was 154 and expected to increase slowly.

This male kakapo, which lives on Codfish Island in New Zealand, is one of fewer than two hundred members of the species. When protected from predators, kakapos can live almost as long as people do.

are free from predators such as dogs and pigs. The largest population is on Stephens Island (known also by the Maori name Takapourewa), where thirty thousand to fifty thousand tuatara live. In 1895 the New Zealand government made it illegal for people to hunt tuatara. These days, mainly biologists visit these reptiles at their isolated island homes.

TUATARA LONGEVITY

Biologists became interested in tuatara for their long life span. They live much longer than many similar creatures, such as lizards, snakes, and other lizardlike reptiles. They live longer than the average human too.

Rumors about tuatara longevity began spreading in the late nineteenth century. Then British naturalist James Hector, who was studying New Zealand's animals and plants, reported that "Maori had knowledge of a tuatara living for many years in a specific location—for 'three generations' was the phrase used," explains Alison Cree, professor and tuatara researcher at the University of Otago in New Zealand. "This statement seems to have been misinterpreted later to mean 'three centuries,' a popular myth."

Yet no one made a scientific study of the tuatara life span until the late 1940s. Then zoologist Bill Dawbin of Victoria University of Wellington began capturing, marking, and releasing tuatara on Stephens Island. He used an identification method common at the time—toe clipping. He removed portions of each animal's toes in a specific pattern, which caused short-term pain but no permanent injuries to the animals. Dawbin returned repeatedly to the island until 1981, recapturing and measuring the growth of the tuatara he had marked. Over the thirty-year period, Dawbin observed the animals' growth rates, from which he and his team could determine age. They found that tuatara reach sexual maturity at about ten to fifteen years, continue growing until they are thirty, and then die at about sixty or seventy. Dawbin died in the late 1990s, and Cree and other tuatara researchers continue finding tuatara that he had marked.

JONATHAN

Tuatara are not the only old reptiles around. Native to the Galapágos Islands off the coast of Ecuador in South America and the Aldabra Atoll near Tanzania in East Africa are the largest tortoises in the world. In the wild, these reptiles, which can weigh up to 550 pounds (250 kg), lumber slowly during their extremely long lives of one hundred years or more.

Reports of even older giant tortoises come from places where they live in captivity. One of the oldest reported is a giant tortoise that spends his days strolling the lawn of Plantation House on the small island of Saint Helena in the South Atlantic Ocean. In the 1930s, Spencer Davis, a British governor of the island, named the tortoise Jonathan.

Officials from the Aldabra Atoll, another British territory, had sent Jonathan to Saint Helena in 1882 as a gift for an earlier British governor. The tortoise was estimated to be about fifty. A photo from around 1886 shows Jonathan at 48 inches (1.2 m) long. (He hasn't grown any longer since.) If Jonathan (*below*) was indeed 50 in 1882, then he was 185 years old in 2017. That makes him the oldest known land animal on Earth.

BACK TO THE MAINLAND

Tuatara are making a comeback on New Zealand's South Island, one of the nation's two main islands. In 2012 Cree and other researchers released eighty-seven tuatara in the Orokonui Ecosanctuary in the southern part of the island. "This was the first such reintroduction of tuatara into the South Island, and we've been following the fates of those animals," Cree says. Both young and old tuatara are surviving at the reserve, where large-area, secure fencing keeps out mammals that prey on the reptile. Workers at the sanctuary have killed or moved other tuatara predators out of the sanctuary. Without predators, tuatara have a chance to survive.

Cree and PhD student Scott Jarvie are tracking this introduced population. They use different methods to observe the tuatara population at Orokonui. They watch them at night, when tuatara hunt for insects and other food. During the day, when tuatara are inside their burrows, Cree and Jarvie look into the burrows with small cameras mounted on the end of long, flexible tubes. They also fit some tuatara with harnesses equipped with radio transmitters and monitor the radio signals to track the animals' movements. Cree and Jarvie even recruit the visiting public to report any tuatara sightings in the sanctuary. Cree hopes that they "will have evidence within a few years that tuatara are reproducing at Orokonui and that the population will thrive there in the longer term."

Alison Cree releases a tuatara into the wild at Orokonui Ecosanctuary on New Zealand's South Island. Local Maori people have supported efforts to protect the tuatara there.

So tuatara may live even longer than Dawbin's estimate. "Recaptures of these animals suggest that a life span of about one hundred years in the wild is possible," says Cree.

NEWER DATING METHODS

Researchers are trying new methods to determine tuatara life spans. In one approach, they insert a tiny electronic microchip encased in a glass tube under a tuatara's skin. Called a passive integrated transponder, the 0.5-inch (1.3 cm) device can be scanned like a bar code. Each tuatara has a unique code, enabling researchers to track individuals' life spans. One of Cree's students is developing an identification method that uses pattern recognition software to find unique skin markings in photographs of tuatara. The method might not be useful, however, because biologists don't know whether markings on tuatara skin are stable throughout their lives. Cree suspects that some of them are, but since tuatara live so long, it will take many years to monitor the markings to know for sure.

Skeletochronology can determine the life span of dead tuatara. With this technique, researchers slice through bones from the toes or legs of dead tuatara. They stain the bone samples to make their markings stand out and, under a microscope, look for rings in the cross sections. Cree says that "these rings, or 'lines of arrested growth,' are likely to form annually, like the rings of tree trunks. Using this approach . . . researchers [estimate] that tuatara [have] a potential life span of at least sixty years."

Tuatara researchers must look at the long-term data collected over the careers of many different biologists. Building upon the discoveries of others leads to a more complete picture of this reptile's long life. Cree says, "It's humbling to work on animals that, in my second half century, may still be older than I am. It's a special moment when you pick up a tuatara . . . that you know you or another researcher held several decades ago."

CHAPTER 6

PANDO AND KING CLONE: PERSISTENT PLANTS

Some of the oldest organisms on Earth are plants. They resist fire, drought, extreme temperatures, invading fungi, and insect and animal attacks to survive for thousands of years. Among the toughest of these longevity masters are some woody trees and bushes that under the right environmental conditions never stop growing.

OLD INDIVIDUALS

The giant sequoias of California are the largest trees on the planet and among the oldest. One of the biggest of these giants is nicknamed General Sherman, after General William Tecumseh Sherman, who led Union troops during the Civil War (1861–1865). At 275 feet (83 m), almost as tall as the Statue of Liberty, General Sherman dwarfs the surrounding trees in Sequoia National Park.

Inyo National Forest in California is home to a number of ancient bristlecone pine trees, including this one. The oldest, named Methuselah, is almost forty-eight hundred years old. Forest officials let people hike near Methuselah and other old bristlecone pines, but they don't identify Methuselah specifically in case anyone would deliberately try to harm it.

General Sherman is not only large—it is also ancient. Botanists can determine a tree's age by dendrochronology, or counting the rings growing around its core, at the very center of its trunk. A new ring grows each year. It's easy to date a tree after it has been cut down. You count the rings running across its stump. Since General Sherman is alive, it can't be dated this easily. Instead, botanists have dated General Sherman by examining samples cut from its trunk combined with ring measurements from stumps of giant sequoias of similar size. Botanists estimate General Sherman to be around 2,150 years old.

Twisted and gnarled bristlecone pine trees are even older than giant sequoias. With their scars and weathering, they look barely alive. Yet they are true survivors, enduring the harsh mountainous conditions in parts of the western United States, where many have grown for

Aboveground, these quaking aspens in Utah's Fishlake National Forest appear to be individual trees. But their roots are all connected belowground. The trees are all part of a single organism.

thousands of years. The oldest yet discovered, living in the White Mountains of eastern California, is called Methuselah, named after the oldest person described in the Bible. Botanists estimate the tree to be about 4,765 years old.

FINDING PANDO

General Sherman and Methuselah are individual trees that have lived thousands of years. But some trees are much older, and they don't grow individually. They are part of a network of trees that grow as a system. One of the largest and oldest tree systems in the world was discovered in the 1970s in Utah. It is a quaking aspen system, and it is immense.

In spring and summer, the trembling leaves of quaking aspen trees flicker in the sunlight, sparkling like forest jewels. Their white trunks gracefully reach toward the sky. But it is the trees' striking fall colors that make them stand out from the dark green sea of evergreens among which they grow. The gold, yellow, and red aspen leaves also reveal the aspens' biggest secret. If you watch the thousands of aspen trees in a forest during the fall, you will see many of them change color at the same time. Those that change color together are all part of one giant clone, a connected system of trees.

Aboveground, the aspens look like individual trees. But underground it's another story: the trees share one root system. Most trees reproduce sexually—their flowers contain both male and female parts. When pollen, or male reproductive cells, fertilizes a tree's female reproductive cells, seeds develop inside the flower. The seeds eventually drop into the soil below, take root, and grow into new trees. But

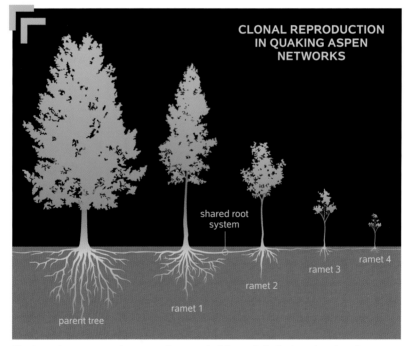

**CLONAL REPRODUCTION
IN QUAKING ASPEN
NETWORKS**

shared root
system

ramet 4

ramet 3

ramet 2

ramet 1

parent tree

The trees in an aspen clone are all connected through their shared root system. They all grow from a single parent plant and are genetically identical.

quaking aspens mostly reproduce asexually. Only the parent tree grows from a seed. From that original tree, shoots called ramets sprout from the organism's roots. They develop into aspen trees that are genetically identical to the parent plant and one another, growing to be about 100 feet (31 m) tall. Individual ramets commonly die after 100 to 150 years, but the system is still alive. To continue to thrive, aspen clone systems depend on continuous growth of new ramets.

In 1975 University of Michigan biologist Burton V. Barnes was studying leaf and bark patterns on aspen trees in southern Utah's Fishlake National Forest. Looking at the trees in aerial photographs, he suspected that they were all part of one big clone. (Genetic testing in 2008 proved this to be true.)

In 1992 University of Colorado biologist Michael C. Grant

nicknamed the clone Pando, which is Latin for "I spread." Pando has an estimated forty-seven thousand ramets. This single organism covers 106 acres (43 ha) of land. Incredibly, this massive clone has grown from a single seed the size of a grain of pepper.

Later in the 1990s, Grant and fellow University of Colorado biologists Jeffry Mitton and Yan Linhart calculated Pando's weight. They had read news stories about a 1,500-acre (607 ha) fungus in southwestern Washington. A group of researchers claimed that it was the largest organism on Earth. Grant, Mitton, and Linhart knew that Pando wasn't as big as the fungus in acreage, but they believed that it weighed more. To find its weight, they estimated the weight of an individual tree and its part of the root system to be 287 pounds (130 kg). Pando has about forty-seven thousand ramets. Multiplying 287 by 47,000, the biologists came up with a total weight of more than 13 million pounds (5.8 million kg)—fifteen times heavier than the fungus. This meant that Pando was the most massive single organism ever found on Earth.

Pando could only have reached such a size over a long period of time. But it's impossible to know precisely when Pando began growing from its original seed. Pando's living trees are all less than 150 years old. The parent tree died and rotted long ago, so its wood cannot be dated. Grant believes that "a reasonable guess [of when Pando began growing] is about fifty thousand to eighty thousand years ago, but some have speculated ten times that age."

A 2017 study provides a much more conservative estimate of Pando's age. The authors of the study looked at the history of glaciers in North America. During the last ice age, which ended about ten thousand years ago, glaciers covered vast areas of Earth, including lands that would become Utah. According to the study authors, Pando could not have grown in Utah when the land was covered by ice. They believe the clone couldn't have started to grow earlier than fourteen thousand years ago, which is when glaciers began to retreat from North America.

THE SOCIAL LIVES OF TREES

Clonal trees such as quaking aspens populate large areas of land, while their shared root system connects them all. Botanists have found that individual trees in a clone can work together for the survival of the entire system. They can send water and nutrients to one another through their roots.

But nonclonal trees cooperate and even communicate with one another. For instance, if insects are attacking one tree, it might emit a hormone that signals other trees to the danger. In response, these trees might emit different chemicals that repel the bugs.

Peter Wohlleben, who works as a government forester in Germany, explains that this communication network also takes place underground. Many trees thrive with the aid of fungi that live on their roots. The fungi derive energy from the trees and in turn provide trees with water and nutrients from the soil. The fungi can also transmit chemical signals from the roots of one tree to the roots of another. Some botanists call this underground network the Wood Wide Web.

German arborist Peter Wohlleben wrote the 2016 surprise best seller *The Hidden Life of Trees*. The book explains how tree roots communicate with one another through a belowground fungal network.

After that, with warmer weather and no glaciers, Pando would have been able to survive.

PANDO IN PERIL

Walking through the Pando clone is easy, like stepping between the columns of an ancient temple. Almost all the trees are fully grown, with very few young trees. Paul Rogers, director of the Western Aspen Alliance, an organization focused on aspen tree science and conservation, says that Pando "looks really pretty and nice, until you realize that it's a very unnatural situation where just the older trees exist." Pando's health depends on continuous new growth. Without new ramets, Pando will die.

What's happening? Why isn't Pando producing new ramets? Botanists have a few theories. One is that wildlife has been eating new ramets before they are established. Another theory is that the forest hasn't had enough wildfires. A wildfire's destruction of individual aspen trees stimulates the clonal root system to send up new ramets. But since people live near Pando and use the forest for recreation, such as bird-watching, hiking, and fishing, the US Forest Service fights and extinguishes any wildfires that break out there.

To test what could best stimulate Pando's growth, Rogers worked with Fishlake National Forest to set up a 15-acre (6 ha) fenced area within the clone. He divided the area into twenty-seven separate plots. The fencing kept out cattle and deer, both of which graze on young tree shoots. Rogers experimented with burning, cutting, and clearing plants within the forest (both aspen trees and other plants) to see how these activities affected the clone's new growth. Over a three-year test period, Rogers found that keeping out deer and cattle had the best results. Without these animals, Pando began producing healthy new ramets.

Deer are abundant in the Pando region, and Rogers explains why. First, local law limits deer hunting. And deer's natural predators—

"THAT GREAT WONDER OF THE WORLD"

Paul Rogers (*below*) is a biogeographer, a combination of a biologist and a geographer. He studies plants, why they grow where they do, and wildfire science. He is especially drawn to quaking aspens because of their beauty and their relationship with fire. He wanted to know more about this "tree that likes fire." He began studying quaking aspens while working for the US Forest Service and traveling around western states to conduct forest surveys. After that, Rogers earned his PhD at Utah State University and joined the faculty there. He started the Western Aspen Alliance and became its director in 2008. He is one of the few active researchers and conservationists working with Pando.

Being inside the Pando clone has given Rogers an even deeper understanding of its ecological importance. "I've spent a lot of time there," he says, "and there's a spiritual beauty to being there, particularly when I'm by myself in that thing that's so immense and seen so much over time. Being in that great wonder of the world is very humbling. It puts you in your place in a sense, making you feel very much a part of the world instead of separated from it. You also feel small, but in a good way."

wolves, bears, and cougars—are not abundant in the area. So the deer population has exploded, and the deer eat ramets. "The excess of these animals cause ecosystems to go out of balance. The most obvious one in the Pando clone is [deer grazing on] the young trees, and so you start to lose generations," explains Rogers. And if Pando goes, many other species that depend on the trees—such as lichen that grow on their bark, flowering plants growing on the forest floor underneath their canopies, and birds that nest in holes inside their trunks—will go with it. To prevent such destruction, the US Forest Service has erected additional 8-foot (2.5 m) fences to keep out deer and other grazing animals. By 2018 fences protected about half of the clone. Rogers is calling attention to Pando's dire situation and hopes for a solution before this ancient aspen clone "comes apart on our watch."

CREOSOTE RINGS

To the untrained eye, a common plant in the Mojave Desert of Southern California doesn't look particularly special. It's not big or beautiful, but the creosote bush knows how to survive in the harshest of desert conditions.

During a field trip in the Mojave in the early 1970s, a student asked Professor Frank C. Vasek of the University of California–Riverside how old the creosote bushes were. He guessed they might be

Hyrum Johnson, a botanist from the University of California–Riverside, collects leaves from creosote bushes in the Mojave Desert. The UC–Riverside team discovered that creosote bushes grow as ring-shaped clones. They named the largest ring King Clone.

BIOLOGICAL BLUEPRINT: KING CLONE

Common name: creosote bush

Scientific name: *Larrea tridentata*

Habitat: King Clone in the Mojave Desert, creosote bushes elsewhere in North America and in South America

Size: 75 x 25 feet (23 x 7.6 m)

Weight: unknown

Life span: estimated 11,700 years old

Curious adaptation: Creosote bushes grow in some of the driest areas of the Americas, where just 3 to 4 inches (8–10 cm) of rain fall each year. So the bush has evolved to survive with very little water. Its leaves are efficient at storing what little water they do get. They can also carry out photosynthesis with very little water. During extreme droughts, a creosote bush sheds its leaves and some of its stems. The plant no longer needs to supply water to these structures, so it can get by on what little water it has stored in its roots. The leaves and stems grow back when water supplies increase.

three hundred to four hundred years old. But then "it suddenly dawned on me that I and everyone else simply did not know," Vasek said. So he and a team of students began studying the creosote bush.

When the team rode in a helicopter to look at the plants from the air, they noticed right away that groups of bushes were shaped into oval rings. "[The rings] are very difficult to detect at ground level but become very clear when you look . . . from a higher altitude," explains Leonel Sternberg, one of Vasek's former students. The ring shapes showed that the bushes were likely part of a clonal system. To find out, Sternberg tested proteins from the bushes. The tests would indicate if the bushes came from the same or different seeds. The tests proved that bushes within the same ring were "genetically identical and therefore clonal," says Sternberg.

Vasek pieced together a possible explanation for how the creosote bush forms a clonal ring. He suspected that after forty to ninety years, the parent plant splits into lobes that form a circle around the parent. These lobes grow roots and live independently of the parent, which eventually dies. Like the parent plant, the young plants also eventually split into lobes. Because the new plants grow outward, away from the original parent plant, the ring of bushes grows larger and larger.

DISCOVERING KING CLONE

Vasek retrieved a piece of wood from inside one creosote bush ring to figure out its age. The wood came from the center of the ring, where plants were no longer living. They had died much earlier in the clone's lifetime. Vasek used carbon 14 dating to determine the age of the wood. What he found was quite surprising. The wood was 585 years old, with a margin of error of plus or minus 150 years. That meant the

This photo clearly shows the ring shape of a creosote clone.

CARBON 14 DATING

To date living and once living things, researchers use several types of carbon 14 dating. One method is often used to date old bones and wood. While they are living, plants and animals take in carbon 14. Plants absorb it from the air, and animals get it from the plants they eat. After death, organisms no longer take in carbon 14. Over time, the carbon 14 remaining in their tissues decays and turns into nitrogen. The decay happens at a constant, known rate.

To measure the age of old bones, wood, and other once living material, researchers measure the carbon 14 remaining in the tissue. Since they know how quickly carbon 14 decays, they can use this measurement to determine how long ago the organism died.

clone had started growing at least 435 years before. But it might have been much older.

The researchers next looked for larger rings to see if they could find even older creosote clones. They used a "high-altitude aerial photo of the area, where we could see many ring forms, and we picked . . . the largest [clone] around this area," Sternberg recalled. When Sternberg and his colleagues got close to the giant ring, they quickly named it King Clone in "appreciation of how big this ring was."

They then took samples from King Clone and carbon-dated the wood. They also compared King Clone's diameter—75 × 25 feet (23 × 7.6 m)—to the rate at which creosote bushes grow. The tests and calculations showed that King Clone was roughly 11,700 years old.

The giant, old creosote ring was growing on privately owned land that was about to be cleared for buildings. So Vasek campaigned to protect King Clone, and in 1985, the State of California acquired the land. It became the King Clone Ecological Reserve in 1993. The California Department of Fish and Wildlife owns the land and doesn't allow development there.

In thinking about his work, Vasek recalled that he had seen creosote bushes growing in the desert many times. He thought of them only as something that "fill[ed] up desert space between the times and places when the 'real' desert plants put on a show of flowers." He never thought much about the plant until a student asked a seemingly simple question about its age. After his discovery of the creosote bush's longevity, Vasek realized, "Sometimes amazing botanical wonders are evident but unnoticed, beneath our very noses."

CHAPTER 7

INSIDE DNA: SEARCHING FOR LONGEVITY GENES

A lizardlike reptile that lives one hundred years, an Arctic shark that lives for three centuries or more, and a clam that's even older than that. The list of longevity masters keeps growing as researchers make new and incredible discoveries. The long life spans are not only astounding, but they also bring up fundamental questions about life and death and how long-lived creatures combat aging.

BABY BOOM

First described by British naturalist Charles Darwin in 1859, natural selection is the process by which animals that are best suited to their environment are most likely to have children. The offspring are also well suited to their environment. They survive and have more children, while animals that are unsuited to their environment die out. Natural selection also explains why some

Mice need to reproduce quickly—before they fall prey to a hawk or other raptor. Their lives are short. Once they have passed on their genes through reproduction, they age and die.

animals and plants have very short lives and others live longer.

Prey animals, such as rodents that are eaten by owls and other big birds, need to reproduce quickly. If they don't have offspring early in life, they might have no offspring. A species that doesn't produce enough offspring is at high risk of extinction. So to ensure that their species live on, many prey animals have evolved to have children early in life. They come to sexual maturity quickly, reproduce quickly, and die after a short time.

But animals that are large and strong or that have protections such as hard shells or the ability to fly away from danger are less vulnerable to predators. For these organisms, reproduction doesn't have to happen in a hurry. It can occur later in life. So these types of animals have evolved to have children later and to live longer.

After an animal's offspring are born, its body can age and die. The animal has successfully passed on its genes, so its evolutionary purpose has been fulfilled. There's no biological purpose to living any longer. Steven N. Austad explains, "Reproduction is the name of the game.

Basically, we age because it's not in nature's best interest to perfectly repair our bodies. The main thing is to keep us reproductive as long as possible, and then let our bodies deteriorate."

THE RATE-OF-LIVING THEORY

An idea called the rate-of-living theory was once popular with biologists. The theory relates to metabolic rate, the rate at which animals convert food to energy inside their cells.

Many large, slow creatures, such as bowhead whales, live longer than smaller, faster creatures, such as mice. Smaller animals have much faster metabolisms: they move and breathe faster than bigger animals. Even their hearts beat faster. The faster they use energy, the faster their bodies produce harmful by-products, such as free radicals, which damage cells. According to the rate-of-living theory, this causes the bodies of smaller animals to break down faster too. And the more damage that occurs in their cells, the theory says, the faster they age.

But bats and naked mole rats poke holes in this theory— they just don't fit. Other animals of their size, such as mice and rats, live a maximum of four to five years. Little brown bats, which are smaller than mice, live decades: twenty-two species

The rate-of-living theory says that small animals, with their fast metabolisms, live short lives. But little brown bats can live for several decades, showing that the rate-of-living theory is incorrect.

live up to twenty years, two species live thirty years, and one species— Brandt's bat—can live more than forty years. And naked mole rats live into their twenties. This and other evidence that animals with fast metabolisms don't necessarily have short lives has put the rate-of-living theory to rest.

THE PROCESSES OF AGING

What exactly happens when people and other animals age? Much of aging starts within cells. Throughout life, oxidative stress occurs deep within mitochondria—the energy-producing organelles (small organs) within every cell. The mitochondria's main job is to turn nutrients and oxygen into adenosine triphosphate (ATP), a form of chemical energy. The organelles also make a by-product: free oxygen radicals, or oxidants.

Oxidants are unstable molecules that break apart other molecules, making them unstable too. This instability causes a chain reaction of damage inside cells. Humans and other animals have some defenses against the damage, such as enzymes (molecules that speed up chemical reactions) that neutralize oxidants. But these defenses can fail, and damage can build up over time. Researchers have found that the damage related to oxidant accumulation increases with age.

Bodies also deteriorate when glucose, or blood sugar, attaches to proteins in the body to form harmful protein clumps. Over time, the accumulated clumps stiffen joints, clog arteries, and form gluey masses between nerve cells in the brain. Protein clumps in the brain cause Alzheimer's disease.

Cell division plays a part in aging too. This division is a normal part of cell growth and repair. Cells divide to make new cells, which replace old, dead, or damaged cells. Chemical signals in the body control most cell division. Biologists believe that as humans and animals age, the control of cell division becomes weaker. When cells are no longer able to stop dividing, cancer can develop. The unregulated dividing cells form cancerous tumors that can invade other parts of the body, destroy healthy tissue, and damage and destroy organs.

Humans have a high cancer rate. In 2012, 14.1 million people around the world had cancer. That number is expected to grow to 24 million by 2035. Although some young people develop cancer, the disease is primarily associated with aging.

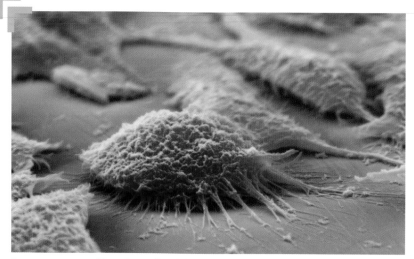

As a person ages, his or her cells might begin to divide uncontrollably. They can become cancerous tumors that destroy healthy tissue. This color-enhanced microscopic image shows a breast cancer cell.

SCOURING ANIMAL DNA

How do long-lived animals fit into the aging picture? They are especially interesting to researchers because they seem to have aging protection and cell-repair mechanisms encoded in their DNA. Geneticists are searching through the genomes (sequences, or maps, of all the genes in a single being) of these longevity masters. They are looking for genes associated with aging and trying to find out how they work.

At the Institute of Ageing and Chronic Disease at the University of Liverpool in England, a team led by geneticist João Pedro de Magalhães mapped the bowhead whale genome and published their results in 2015. Humans have 37.2 trillion cells, and bowhead whales have more than one thousand times that. According to Magalhães, more cells should logically increase the chance of the uncontrollable cell division that leads to cancer. Yet the whales "do not exhibit an increased cancer risk, suggesting the existence of natural mechanisms that can suppress cancer more effectively in these animals," he explains.

Magalhães's team compared the bowhead's genome with genomes of similar animals, such as the minke whale and the dolphin, searching for genes that stood out. What they discovered were "[differences] in bowhead genes related to cell cycle, DNA repair, cancer, and aging." Magalhães has also studied the genome of the naked mole rat, which has a far longer life span than other rats. He found genes that might be important to the rats' longer life span and to their resistance to cancer. Magalhães thinks that "different species can have different [biological] tricks to have a long life span, so we should study multiple long-lived, disease-resistant species."

The Greenland shark's longevity tricks may be hidden in its DNA too. Evolutionary biologist Kim Praebel and others from the Norwegian College of Fishery Science in Tromsø, Norway, are trying to find out what those tricks might be. They have mapped the mitochondrial DNA (DNA found in mitochondria) of one hundred Greenland sharks. They are also mapping and analyzing the complete genomes of two hundred other Greenland sharks. For their tests, they used DNA samples from skin on Greenland shark fins provided by Julius Nielsen and his team. One of the goals of Praebel's studies is to find the genes that direct the sharks' long life spans. He says, "If we can identify the genes and the [cellular] processes that are involved in determining life span [and] longevity, we would have made a groundbreaking discovery that would have wide-ranging applications in biology, conservation, and medicine."

LONGEVITY LESSONS

If we can figure out why certain animals live so long, Magalhães says, we might learn "the secret for living longer, healthier lives and may be able to apply this knowledge to improve human health and preserve human life." We might even be able to create medicines that slow or reverse aging. Magalhães says he is "optimistic about the development of longevity drugs" and is "convinced that we will see longevity drugs becoming widespread [by about 2040]." Researchers are already developing and testing such drugs. In one 2017 study, biologists at the Erasmus University Medical Center in the Netherlands injected old mice with peptides, a type

LONGEVITY GENES

The first longevity gene that researchers discovered belongs to a tiny worm called *Caenorhabditis elegans*, or *C. elegans* for short. This worm normally lives only a few days in the wild, but it can live up to three weeks in the ideal conditions of a laboratory. In the 1980s, University of California–Riverside geneticists Tom Johnson and David Friedman launched a study. They observed groups of *C. elegans*, identified them, and isolated the longest living of the worms. In the lab, the longer-living worms reproduced, and their offspring were also long-lived. After eighteen generations, the worms were living much longer than their ancestors and most other *C. elegans*.

This study showed that longevity can be inherited and that genes are likely responsible for the long life spans. Johnson and Friedman eventually found the longevity gene for *C. elegans*. They called it age-1. In their study, worms with the age-1 gene lived 65 percent longer than the average *C. elegans*.

In 1993 Cynthia Kenyon, a geneticist at the University of California–San Francisco, also studied the genes of *C. elegans*. She found a gene called daf-2 that seems to be involved in aging. Using genetic engineering—or manipulating genes in a laboratory—Kenyon disabled this gene in certain worms. "Switching off" this gene more than doubled a worm's life.

of amino acid. The peptides targeted and destroyed frail and damaged cells in the old mice. After four weeks of being treated, the mice's coats turned from scraggly and dull to full and shiny, their kidneys and livers started working more efficiently, and their energy levels increased dramatically. The research team plans to test the same drug on humans.

It is highly unlikely that anyone will become immortal because of longevity drugs. But such drugs could possibly add years to a person's life while also improving health.

WHAT'S NEXT?

Discovering creatures with long life spans, from the immortal jellyfish to glass sponge reefs, sometimes happens by accident. But these discoveries are just the beginning. They lead to many more questions, such as, What other creatures can outlive humans? What longevity masters are yet to be discovered? And what can they teach us about human aging and longevity? Will these secrets lead to improved, longer lives for humans?

Researchers are working on all these questions. What we do know is that extraordinary life—whether long-lived or not—surrounds us all, inconspicuously thriving right underneath our noses.

CURIOUSLY RESILIENT: THE NAKED MOLE RAT

Wrinkled, pink, and pretty much hairless—with two large front teeth—the naked mole rat (*right*) is an unusual-looking animal. The tiny rodent is also unusual in its extreme longevity. It can live more than thirty years—about ten times longer than mice, which are about the same size. Biologist Rochelle Buffenstein, who works

for a biotech company in San Francisco, California, has studied naked mole rats for more than thirty years. She notes that these rodents are resistant to many problems of aging, including cancer, diabetes, heart and brain diseases, and many types of infections. They can even survive up to eighteen minutes without oxygen.

In most mammals, the risk of death increases at a certain rate after they reach sexual maturity. In humans, this risk doubles every eight years after age thirty. But Buffenstein's data show something very different for naked mole rats. After they reach sexual maturity (at six months), their chances of dying stay the same for the rest of their lives.

Scientists who study aging want to know more about the naked mole rat. Does its extreme longevity rest in its DNA or in its cells' ability to repair themselves? Only more studies will reveal the answers.

COMPARATIVE TIMELINE

What was happening in history when some of the longest-living organisms were born?

HISTORIC MARKERS	APPROXIMATE TIME	LIVING THINGS
Woolly mammoths, saber-toothed cats, and giant short-faced bears live in ice-free areas of North America.	14,000 to 11,000 years ago	The Pando quaking aspen clone possibly starts growing in Utah.
Humans in some parts of Earth begin farming.	11,700 years ago	King Clone, a clonal ring of the creosote bush, starts growing in the Mojave Desert.
Catalhuyuk, one of the world's first cities, develops in Turkey.	9,000 years ago	The glass sponge reefs off the western coast of Canada begin forming.
The ancient Egyptian civilization thrives in North Africa.	4,765 years ago	Methuselah the bristlecone pine tree begins growing in California.
The Phoenicians, a Middle Eastern culture, develop a twenty-two-letter alphabet.	3,000 years ago	The stromatolites in the Bahamas and in Shark Bay, Australia, start forming.
The Nazca civilization develops in Peru.	2,150 years ago	The giant sequoia tree called General Sherman begins growing in California.
The Ming dynasty rules in China.	1499	Ming the quahog is born.
Europeans explore and establish colonies in North America.	1500s to 1730s	The oldest Greenland shark in a 2016 study is born.
The commercial whaling industry thrives.	1600s through 1800s	Some individual glass sponges in reefs off the western coast of Canada begin growing.
American colonists battle Britain to win their independence during the American Revolution.	1770s	The oldest bowhead whale in a 1999 study is born.
Charles Darwin works as a naturalist aboard the HMS *Beagle*.	1832	Jonathan the giant tortoise is born.
Americans buy the first mass-produced automobiles.	1910s	Some of the oldest living tuatara are born.

SOURCE NOTES

12 Erin Conroy, "Netted Whale Hit by Lance a Century Ago," *NBC News*, last modified June 12, 2007, http://www.nbcnews .com/id/19195624/ns/technology _and_science-science/t/netted -whale-hit-lance-century-ago /#.WQojzBg-JUQ.

16 Amanda Leigh Haag, "Patented Harpoon Pins Down Whale Age," *Nature*, June 19, 2007, http://www.nature.com/news /2007/070619/full/news070618 -6.html.

19 Ibid.

22 Mads Peter Heide-Jørgensen, interview with author, March 15, 2017.

22 Ibid.

23 Haag, "Patented Harpoon Pins."

23 Ibid.

26 Julius Nielsen, interview with author, March 20, 2017.

28 Ibid.

28 Ibid.

28 Ibid.

28 Ibid.

29 Ibid.

29–30 Ibid.

30 Ibid.

31 Ibid.

31 Ibid.

32 Steven N. Austad, interview with author, March 13, 2017.

32 Ibid.

38 Daniel Martinez, interview with author, June 8, 2017.

38 Ibid.

40 Ibid.

41 Ibid.

41 Ibid.

42 Ibid.

43 Ibid.

46 Ferdinando Boero, interview with author, April 18, 2017.

46 Ibid.

47 Nathaniel Rich, "Can a Jellyfish Unlock the Secret of Immortality?," *New York Times*, November 28, 2012.

47 Boero, interview.

51 "Protecting the Glass Sponge Reefs," Canadian Parks and Wilderness Society, accessed October 26, 2017, http:// glassspongereefs.com /conservation/.

54 Sally Leys, interview with author, May 5, 2017.

54 Ibid.

55 Ibid.

55 Pamela Reid, interview with author, June 6, 2017.

57 Ibid.

57 Ibid.

58 Ibid.

58 Ibid.

61 Ibid.

66 Alison Cree, interview with author, June 15, 2017.

68 Alison Cree, interview with author, July 25, 2017.

68 Michael Grant, interview with author, May 28, 2017.

69 Cree, interview, June 15, 2017.

69 Ibid.

69 Ibid.

75 Paul Rogers, interview with author, May 19, 2017.

77 Ibid.

78 Ibid.

78 Ibid.

78 Ibid.

79 Sandra Blakeslee, "After 11,700 Years, World's Oldest Known Plant Gains Refuge," *New York Times*, February 24, 1985, http:// www.nytimes.com/1985/02/24 /us/after-11700-years-world -s-oldest-known-plant-gains -refuge.html.

80 Leonel Sternberg, interview with author, May 4, 2017.

80 Ibid.

82 Blakeslee, "After 11,700 Years."

83 Rogers, interview.

85–86 João Pedro de Magalhães, interview with author, April 30, 2017.

88 Ibid.

89 Ibid.

89 Kim Praebel, interview with author, August 22, 2017.

89 Magalhães, interview.

89 Ibid.

GLOSSARY

baleen: a substance found in stiff plates that hang from the upper jaws of whales without teeth. Whales use the comblike plates to strain small creatures from ocean water for food.

bomb pulse: a spike in carbon 14 levels in Earth's atmosphere resulting from aboveground nuclear bomb tests in the 1950s and early 1960s. Plants absorbed the excess carbon 14 from the atmosphere, and animals absorbed it by eating plants and smaller animals that fed on plants. Biologists measure carbon 14 levels in the eye lenses of Greenland sharks to determine whether they were born before or after the bomb pulse.

carbon 14 dating: also called radiocarbon dating, a technique for determining the age of once living things. Plants and animals absorb carbon 14 when they are alive and stop absorbing it after death. Archaeologists and other scientists measure carbon 14 levels in fossils and use the known rate of carbon 14 decay to estimate a fossil's age.

carnivore: an animal or plant that feeds on animal tissue

clone: a group of plants that share a single root system and are genetically identical. Some large stands of trees, such as the quaking aspen trees in Utah's Fishlake National Forest, are clones.

cold-blooded: having a body temperature that depends on the temperature of the environment. Most animals are cold-blooded, except for birds and mammals.

cyanobacteria: tiny, single-celled organisms that use photosynthesis to make food. Cyanobacteria are found at the top of stromatolites. They trap sand and minerals that make stromatolites grow taller.

dendrochronology: dating trees and pieces of wood by counting their growth rings

deoxyribonucleic acid (DNA): a molecule found in the cells of all living things. DNA contains the instructions for how each organism will grow, function, and reproduce. Genes are segments of DNA.

ecosystem: a biological community of living things and the environment in which they exist. Members of ecosystems depend on one another for survival. For instance, in a glass sponge reef, octopuses, crabs, and shrimp can stay safe from predators by hiding in the reef's many crevices.

evolution: organisms changing over time, either randomly or in ways that enhance an organism's chances of reproduction and survival. These changes can lead to the development of different species.

extinct: having no living members. A species becomes extinct when the last individual in the species dies.

fossil: the remains or impression of a plant or animal of a past era. Some fossils take the form of rock. They develop when mineral-rich water percolates into dead plant or animal tissue, and the minerals gradually replace the tissue. This process created fossilized glass sponge reefs in Europe.

gene: a segment of DNA that contains information about a certain biological trait or function. Offspring inherit genes from their parents.

genetic engineering: altering the genes of living things using laboratory techniques

glacier: a large mass of ice that moves slowly across the land. Glaciers are made of packed snow that has built up over many years.

hormone: a chemical substance produced by a plant or animal. Some hormones regulate body functions. Others carry messages from one part of the body to another or send messages from one organism to another.

immortal: capable of living forever. Biologists think that *Hydra vulgaris* is immortal because it does not age and its cells can repair themselves endlessly.

mammals: warm-blooded vertebrates (animals with backbones) that possess hair or fur and that nourish their young with milk produced by mammary glands

margin of error: the degree to which a statistic or test result might be inaccurate. For instance, an estimate of a Greenland shark's age might have a margin of error of twenty-nine years, meaning that the shark might be twenty-nine years older or twenty-nine years younger than the estimate.

metabolism: when cells produce the substances and energy needed for life. Small animals have faster metabolisms than larger animals.

metamorphosis: a change in the physical form of an animal as it progresses from birth to adulthood. Many insects and marine animals undergo metamorphosis.

mitochondria: parts of a cell that convert chemical energy into a form of energy that the cell can use. Mitochondria also contain DNA.

natural selection: the process, first described by British naturalist Charles Darwin in 1859, by which organisms that are best adapted to their environment are more likely to survive and produce offspring. These organisms will pass the traits that help them survive on to their offspring. Those organisms that are less well adapted to their environment will die before having children. Their species might die out.

photosynthesis: the process by which green plants, algae, and some other organisms make their own food using energy from the sun and carbon dioxide from the air or water. Photosynthesis produces oxygen as a by-product.

pollen: tiny grains produced in the male organs of plants. Sperm, or male reproductive cells, develop inside pollen. For plants to reproduce, pollen from male organs must travel to female plant organs.

radiocarbon dating: also called carbon 14 dating, a way to determine the age of once living things. Plants and animals absorb carbon 14 when they are alive and stop absorbing it after death. Archaeologists and other scientists measure carbon 14 levels in fossils and use the known rate of carbon 14 decay to estimate a fossil's age.

sonar: a system for locating objects and measuring their speed, distance, and direction using sound waves. Sonar systems send sound waves through the air or water. The waves bounce off objects and return. Sonar systems analyze the returning waves to obtain information about the objects.

stem cells: cells that have the ability to differentiate, or turn into many different cell types. Stem cells constantly renew themselves and can repair and replace tissues in an animal. In most animals, stem cells are only in embryos. But *Hydra vulgaris*'s whole body is made of stem cells.

transdifferentiation: the natural but rare transformation of specialized cells into other kinds of specialized cells. The cells of *Turritopsis dohrnii* are capable of doing this.

undifferentiated cells: cells that are able to turn into any kind of cell for any part of an animal's body. Stem cells are undifferentiated cells.

vertebrate: an animal with a spinal column

warm-blooded: having a body temperature that is regulated internally, not by the temperature of the environment. Birds and mammals are warm-blooded animals.

zooplankton: small animal life that floats in the water. Many larger sea animals, such as bowhead whales, feed on zooplankton.

SELECTED BIBLIOGRAPHY

Austad, Steven N. *Why We Age: What Science Is Discovering about the Body's Journey through Life*. New York: John Wiley & Sons, 1997.

Boero, Ferdinando. "Everlasting Life: The 'Immortal' Jellyfish." *Biologist* 63, no. 3 (2017): 16–19.

Conway, K. W., M. Krautter, J. V. Barrie, and M. Neuweiler. "Hexactinellid Sponge Reefs on the Canadian Continental Shelf: A Unique 'Living Fossil.'" *Geoscience Canada* 28, no. 2 (2001): 71–78.

Cree, Alison. "The Tenacious Tuatara." *Natural History* 123, no. 1 (2015): 22–27.

Daugherty, Charles, and Alison Cree. "Tuatara: A Survivor from the Dinosaur Age." *New Zealand Geographic* 6 (April–June 1990): 66–86.

DeWoody, Jennifer, Carol A. Rowe, Valerie D. Hipkins, and Karen E. Mock. "'Pando' Lives: Molecular Genetic Evidence of a Giant Aspen Clone in Central Utah." *Western North American Naturalist* 68, no. 4 (2008): art. 8.

Ding, C., S. G. Schreiber, D. R. Roberts, A. Hamann, and J. S. Brouard. "Post-glacial Biogeography of Trembling Aspen Inferred from Habitat Models and Genetic Variance in Quantitative Traits." *Scientific Reports* 7 (2017): art. 4672.

George, John C., Jeffrey Bada, Judith Zeh, Laura Scott, Stephen E. Brown, Todd O'Hara, and Robert Suydam. "Age and Growth Estimates of Bowhead Whales (*Balaena mysticetus*) via Aspartic Acid Racemization." *Canadian Journal of Zoology* 77 (1999): 571–580.

Grant, Michael C. "The Trembling Giant." *Discover*, October 1, 1993. http://discovermagazine.com/1993/oct/thetremblinggian285.

Haag, Amanda Leigh. "Patented Harpoon Pins Down Whale Age." *Nature*, June 19, 2007. http://www.nature.com/news/2007/070619/full/news070618-6.html#B1.

Lenhoff, Howard M., and Sylvia G. Lenhoff. "Abraham Trembley and the Origins of Research on Regeneration in Animals." In *A History of Regeneration Research: Milestones in the Evolution of a Science*, edited by Charles E. Dinsmore, 47–52. New York: Cambridge University Press, 1991.

Leys, S. P., and G. O. Mackie. "Electrical Recording from a Glass Sponge." *Nature* 387 (1997): 29–30.

Leys, S. P., G. O. Mackie, and H. M. Reiswig. "The Biology of Glass Sponges." *Advances in Marine Biology* 52 (2007): 3–10.

Nielsen, J., R. B. Hedeholm, J. Heinemeier, P. G. Bushnell, J. S. Christiansen, J. Olsen, C. B. Ramsey et al. "Eye Lens Radiocarbon Reveals Centuries of Longevity in the Greenland Shark (*Somniosus microcephalus*)." *Science* 353, no. 6300 (2016): 702.

Rogers, P. C., and J. A. Gale. "Restoration of the Iconic Pando Aspen Clone: Emerging Evidence of Recovery." *Ecosphere* 8, no. 1 (2017): e01661.

Vasek, Frank C. "Creosote Bush: Long-Lived Clones in the Mojave Desert." *American Journal of Botany* 67, no. 2 (February 1980): 246–255.

FURTHER INFORMATION

BOOKS

Blevins, Wiley. *Ninja Plants: Survival and Adaptation in the Plant World*. Minneapolis: Twenty-First Century Books, 2017.

Cheshire, James. *Where the Animals Go: Tracking Wildlife with Technology in 50 Maps and Graphics*. New York: W. W. Norton, 2017.

Cree, Alison. *Tuatara: Biology and Conservation of a Venerable Survivor*. Christchurch, NZ: Canterbury University Press, 2014.

Downer, Ann. *The Animal Mating Game: The Wacky, Weird World of Sex in the Animal Kingdom*. Minneapolis: Twenty-First Century Books, 2017.

Hirsch, Rebecca E. *De-extinction: The Science of Bringing Lost Species Back to Life*. Minneapolis: Twenty-First Century Books, 2017.

Leis, R. J., and Bruce Stinchcomb. *Stromatolites: Ancient, Beautiful, and Earth-Altering*. Atglen, PA: Schiffer, 2015.

Mitchell, Megan. *The Human Genome*. New York: Cavendish Square, 2017.

Moon, Beth. *Ancient Trees: Portraits of Time*. New York: Abbeville, 2014.

Silvertown, Jonathan. *The Long and the Short of It: The Science of Life Span and Aging*. Chicago: University of Chicago Press, 2013.

Sussman, Rachel. *The Oldest Living Things in the World*. Chicago: University of Chicago Press, 2014.

Wohlleben, Peter. *The Hidden Life of Trees: What They Feel, How They Communicate—Discoveries from a Secret World*. Vancouver: Greystone Books, 2016.

Young, Karen Romero. *Shark Quest: Protecting the Ocean's Top Predators*. Minneapolis: Twenty-First Century Books, 2019.

———. *Whale Quest: Working Together to Save Endangered Species*. Minneapolis: Twenty-First Century Books, 2018.

WEBSITES

Bahamas Marine EcoCentre: Stromatolites
http://www.tropicbirds.org/stromatolites-3/
Learn about the stromatolites of Shark Bay in Australia and the ongoing studies to understand their bacterial communities and growth patterns.

Canadian Parks and Wilderness Society: Sea of Glass
http://glassspongereefs.com
This site focuses on the glass sponge reefs off British Columbia's coast, with information about how they were discovered, how they are studied, and how they are being protected.

North Slope Borough: Bowhead Whales
http://www.north-slope.org/departments/wildlife-management/studies-and
-research-projects/bowhead-whales
At this site are many resources on bowhead whales, including information about
the traditional indigenous hunts in Barrow, Alaska, and the research on whale
tissues provided by these hunters.

Old and Cold: Biology of the Greenland Shark
http://bioold.science.ku.dk/jfsteffensen/OldAndCold/
This project, whose participants include Julius Nielsen, Kim Praebel, and John
Steffensen, involves studying the biology, migration patterns, and genetics of the
Greenland shark. The site includes photos of the team at work.

Orokonui Ecosanctuary
https://orokonui.nz
Visit this site to learn more about the released mainland population of tuatara in
New Zealand and the ecosanctuary where they live.

"Then and Now: The HMS *Challenger* Expedition and the 'Mountains in the Sea'
Expedition"
http://oceanexplorer.noaa.gov/explorations/03mountains/background/challenger
/challenger.html
At this site, visitors can learn about the nineteenth-century HMS Challenger
Expedition, which found many kinds of previously unknown marine life-forms,
including glass sponges.

Western Aspen Alliance
http://western-aspen-alliance.org
Find out more about Pando, the quaking aspen clone in Utah, other quaking
aspen communities, and the conservation work of Paul Rogers, director of the
Western Aspen Alliance.

VIDEOS

"The Animal That Wouldn't Die"
https://www.youtube.com/watch?v=GRNVc2xC2O0
http://www.npr.org/sections/krulwich/2014/09/26/351440526/everything-dies
-right-but-does-everything-have-to-die-here-s-a-surprise
Made by National Public Radio, this short animated film features Daniel
Martinez and his discovery of the hydra's immortality.

Arctic Currents: A Year in the Life of a Bowhead Whale
https://arcticcurrents.wordpress.com/see-the-film/
This animated film, made by the University of Alaska Museum of the North,
shows the bowhead whale's migration across the Arctic.

Children of the Arctic

http://worldchannel.org/programs/episode/arf-s4-e410-children-arctic/

Follow the lives of teenagers living in Barrow, Alaska, as they struggle with their changing ecosystem and keeping their traditions alive in modern America.

Making North America: Life

http://www.pbs.org/wgbh/nova/earth/making-north-america.html#north-america-life

This documentary from the Public Broadcasting Service includes a segment on stromatolites in North America.

"Shin Kubota Sings a Song about Jellyfish"

https://www.youtube.com/watch?v=sTeer-apF0I

Shin Kubota studies how *Turritopsis dohrnii* returns to its polyp stage when it is threatened, which allows it to generate new jellyfish. He also dresses up as Mr. Immortal Jellyfish Man and sings about jellyfish.

"The Story of the Glass Sponge Reefs"

http://momentummediaproductions.com/portfolio/72/

This short film follows an expedition to see the glass sponge reefs off the coast of British Columbia. It includes an appearance by Sally Leys.

INDEX

ABOUT THE AUTHOR

Karen Latchana Kenney writes books about animals, and she looks for them wherever she goes—from leafcutter ants trailing through the Amazon rain forest in Guyana, where she was born, to puffins in cliff-side burrows on the Irish island of Skellig Michael. Kenney enjoys creating books about nature, biodiversity, conservation, and groundbreaking scientific discoveries. Her award-winning and star-reviewed books include *Exoplanets: Worlds beyond Our Solar System*, *Everything World War I*, and *Stephen Hawking: Extraordinary Theoretical Physicist*. She lives in Minneapolis with her husband and son, and she bikes, hikes, and gazes at the night sky in northern Minnesota any moment she can. Visit her online at http://latchanakenney.wordpress.com.

PHOTO ACKNOWLEDGMENTS

Image Credits: © Todd Mintz/naturepl.com, p. 7; The Print Collector/Getty Images, p. 8; Courtesy of the New Bedford Whaling Museum, p. 11; Monique Berger/Biosphoto/Getty Images, p. 13; Manuel Litran/Getty Images, p. 14; © Doug Allan/naturepl.com, p. 17; Laura Westlund/Independent Picture Service, pp. 20, 41, 45, 59, 73; © Franco Banfi/naturepl.com, p. 25; Julius Nielsen, Phd student, University of Copenhagen, pp. 27, 28; Steven N. Austad, p. 32; © Kim Taylor/naturepl.com, pp. 35, 37; ullstein bild/Getty Images, p. 39; Daniel E. Martinez, p. 40; Stefano Piraino, p. 44; The Jellyfish That Holds a Key to Immortality/Motherboard/Youtube, 6 May 2014. P. 47; Courtesy of Sally Leys, University of Alberta, and CSSF, pp. 49, 52; Eugueni Matveev, p. 53; R. Pamela Reid, pp. 56, 58, 61; © Michael and Patricia Fogden/Minden Pictures, p. 63; © Tui De Roy/Minden Pictures, p. 65; GIANLUIGI GUERCIA/AFP/Getty Images, p. 67; Ken Miller, University of Otago, p. 68; hlsnow/iStock/Getty Images, p. 71; Paul C. Rogers, Western Aspen Alliance, pp. 72, 78; Craig Stennett/Alamy Stock Photo, p. 76; Leonel Sternberg, p. 79; DAN SUZIO/Science Source/Getty Images, p. 81; sirtravelalot/Shutterstock.com, p. 85; Gunter Marx Photography/Corbis Documentary/Getty Images, p. 86; Eye of Science/Science Source, p. 88; Mint Images - Frans Lanting/Getty Images, p. 91.

Cover: © Kim Taylor/naturepl.com.